Selda Ozdemir

Attention Deficit Hyperactivity Disorder

Selda Ozdemir

Attention Deficit Hyperactivity Disorder: An Early Intervention Approach for Preventing Social, Emotional, and Academic Problems

Implementation Effectiveness with Children
with Attention Deficit Hyperactivity Disorder

VDM Verlag Dr. Müller

KH

Imprint

Bibliographic information by the German National Library: The German National Library lists this publication at the German National Bibliography; detailed bibliographic information is available on the Internet at http://dnb.d-nb.de.

Cover image: www.purestockx.com
Published 2008 Saarbrücken

Publisher:
VDM Verlag Dr. Müller Aktiengesellschaft & Co. KG, Dudweiler Landstr. 125 a,
66123 Saarbrücken, Germany,
Phone +49 681 9100-698, Fax +49 681 9100-988,
Email: info@vdm-verlag.de
Zugl.: Tempe, Arizona State University, Diss., 2006

Produced in Germany by:
Schaltungsdienst Lange o.H.G., Zehrensdorfer Str. 11, 12277 Berlin, Germany
Books on Demand GmbH, Gutenbergring 53, 22848 Norderstedt, Germany

Impressum

Bibliografische Information der Deutschen Nationalbibliothek: Die Deutsche Nationalbibliothek verzeichnet diese Publikation in der Deutschen Nationalbibliografie; detaillierte bibliografische Daten sind im Internet über http://dnb.d-nb.de abrufbar.

Coverbild: www.purestockx.com
Erscheinungsjahr: 2008
Erscheinungsort: Saarbrücken

Verlag: VDM Verlag Dr. Müller Aktiengesellschaft & Co. KG, Dudweiler Landstr. 125 a,
D- 66123 Saarbrücken,
Telefon +49 681 9100-698, Telefax +49 681 9100-988,
Email: info@vdm-verlag.de
Zugl.: Tempe, Arizona State University, Diss., 2006

Herstellung in Deutschland:
Schaltungsdienst Lange o.H.G., Zehrensdorfer Str. 11, D-12277 Berlin
Books on Demand GmbH, Gutenbergring 53, D-22848 Norderstedt

ISBN: 978-3-8364-7058-2

4/15/13

TABLE OF CONTENTS

iii

iv

CHAPTER I

Introduction

Background of the Problem

AD/HD is the most commonly diagnosed childhood disorder, affecting an estimated 3 to 5 percent of the kindergarten and school-age children in the U.S. (American Psychiatric Association, 1994). Perhaps as a result of such rates, AD/HD has become one of the most extensively researched of all childhood psychiatric disorders (Blachman & Hinshaw, 2002). This prevalence estimate means that almost 1 in every 20 children, or at least 1 child per classroom, is likely to be identified as having AD/HD (McGoey, Eckert, & DuPaul, 2002). Symptoms with regard to attention-deficit/hyperactivity disorder (AD/HD) manifest as long-standing, pervasive, and developmentally severe difficulties in hyperactivity (motoric activity), impulsivity, and inattention (Blachman & Hinshaw, 2002). Secondary features associated with the disorder are also often quite problematic; such difficulties involve aggression, poor peer relations, academic underachievement, learning problems, and low self-esteem and depressive symptoms (Barkley, 1998; Hinshaw, 1994).

Although earlier research has focused primarily on the attentional, academic/learning, and behavioral problems associated with this disorder (Treuting & Hinshaw, 2001), the social-emotional domain is being increasingly accepted as one of critical importance for these youngsters (Mikami & Hinshaw, 2003). The difficulties in the social domain are so common that some investigators have claimed that the phenomenon of disturbed social relations itself should serve as a classifying characteristic of the disorder (Landau & Moore, 1991; Whalen & Henker, 1991). In fact, Erhardt and Hinshaw (1994) argued that social problems of children with AD/HD may be central to an understanding of the psychopathology of these children (Landau, Milich, &

6

Diener, 1998).

Research showed that children with AD/HD have significant problems with emotion regulation (Braaten & Rosen, 2000; Maedgen & Carlson, 2000; Southam-Gerow & Kendall, 2002). According to Barkley (1998), children with AD/HD exhibit 1) greater emotional expression in their reactions to events; (2) less objectivity in the selection of a response to an event; (3) diminished social perspective taking, as these children do not delay their initial emotional reaction long enough to take the view of others and their own needs into account; and (4) diminished ability to induce drive and motivational states in themselves in the service of goal-directed behavior. Limited research in this area has provided preliminary evidence that emotion regulation abilities are modestly related to underlying problems with impulse control and hyperactivity, and also represent a different domain of skills that add incremental information to the prediction of social functioning in children with AD/HD (Melnick & Hinshaw, 2000). Furthermore, Eisenberg and colleagues (1995, 1997) have showed that children's negative emotionality and poor emotion regulation are implicated in the risk for social maladaptation. Children who are able to "keep cool" under emotionally arousing conditions are better able to use competent and peer-oriented solutions that yield interpersonal harmony and cooperation with rules. On the contrary, children who become overstimulated or who deal unconstructively with emotion are likely to behave aggressively, withdraw, and disrupt play (Eisenberg, Fabes, Nyman, Bernzweig, & Pinuelas, 1994). Thus, research on children with AD/HD has revealed that deficits in emotional regulation signify one of the primary areas of impairment in AD/HD which eventually result in various problems in social relationships (Barkley, 1997a).

As a result of complex and multifaceted emotional and behavioral problems, children with AD/HD are severely impaired in the social area and are strongly rejected by their peers (Hinshaw & Melnick, 1995; Whalen & Henker, 1985). In particular, the interpersonal behaviors of children with AD/HD are often described as more impulsive, intrusive, excessive, disorganized, engaging, aggressive, intense, and emotional. Thus they are disruptive of the smoothness of the ongoing stream of social interactions, reciprocity, and cooperation, which is an increasingly essential part of the children's social lives with others (Barkley, 1998). Furthermore, children with AD/HD appear to perceive social and emotional cues from others in a more limited and inaccurate fashion, as if they were not paying as much attention to emotional information provided by others. However, research also showed that they do not differ in terms of their capacity to understand the emotional expressions of other children (Casey, 1996).

It is not surprising then, that children with AD/HD are rejected at higher rates than are their non-AD/HD peers (Johnston, Pelham, & Murphy, 1985). Although peer rejection does not, in itself, indicates an externalizing behavior disorder, it is well known that low social status with peers significantly predicts a host of negative outcomes in later life (Parker & Asher, 1987) and covaries positively with disruptive and particularly aggressive behavior (Erhardt & Hinshaw, 1992). Research has found that children with high ratings in kindergarten on hyperactivity and aggression were more likely than those initially rated average or low on hyperactivity and aggression to have third and fourth grade outcomes of peer rated aggression and self-reported delinquency (Vitaro, Tremblay, Gagnon, & Pelletier, 1994).

It is also interesting to note that, when tracking children diagnosed with AD/HD into adolescence and adulthood, those who ultimately experience the most serious clinical problems (e.g., substance abuse, criminal arrests and incarceration, psychiatric hospitalization) were previously identified as having difficulties with aggression (Hinshaw, 1987) or social relations

8

(Parker & Asher, 1987). Thus, most of these risks seem to be increased further by the coexistence of hostile, conduct disordered behavior patterns, or oppositional defiant disorder (ODD), with early onset hyperactive-impulsive behavior (Anastopoulos, Guevremont, Shelton, & DuPaul, 1992; Stormont-Spurgin & Zentall, 1995).

Interventions for children with AD/HD

The considerable risks posed for young children with early hyperactive-impulsive-inattentive behavior, when combined with early hostile, defiant behavior, clearly justify attempts at early intervention that may diminish or ward off these developmental risks (Shelton et al., 2000). Currently, most professionals argue that children with AD/HD should be treated with a combination of interventions that typically involves stimulant medication along with behavior management in the home and at school (Barkley, 1998; Hinshaw, 1994). However, some professionals are hesitant to medicate young children with AD/HD and instead often suggest behavior management and parent training.

Several programs have already initit to intervene early in the lives of children having disruptive behavior patterns or having other factors that place them at risk for developing later antisocial behavior. These interventions have typically focused on either parent or classroom interventions or a combination of these programs (Shelton et al., 2000). According to Noam & Hermann, (2002) an important dynamic in selecting an intervention for at risk young children is that we specifically need programs placed directly in the natural ecology and developmental context where children grow up and that bridge the different worlds that children inhabit. Thus, research supports the need to expand early intervention efforts beyond the classroom in order to achieve better generalization (Lewis, Sugai, & Colvin, 1998).

There is a clear evidence that effective early intervention programs have the potential to prevent long-term negative outcomes if they are of high quality and are comprehensive in nature (Reid, 1993). Among the few empirically supported early intervention programs for at-risk children for antisocial behaviors, the First Step to Success (FSS) has been shown to be effective in decreasing the number of psychosocial risk factors associated with antisocial behavior and in increasing the overall well-being and adjustment of kindergartners at risk (Kashani, Jones, Bumby, & Thomas, 1999). The FSS was designed to achieve secondary prevention goals with its three main components: kindergarten-wide screening process, the classroom-based CLASS curriculum, and HomeBase, which recruits parents as partners with the school in teaching the at-risk child a behavior pattern contributing to school success and the development of friendships (Walker, Kavanagh, Stiller, Golly, Severson, & Feil, 1998).

Recent investigations have showed that the FSS intervention produced extremely robust effect sizes in the following areas as indicated by teacher ratings and direct observations: adaptive behavior, aggressive behavior, maladaptive behavior, and average percentage of academic engaged time in teacher-assigned tasks (Walker et al., 1998). In addition, evaluation of the social validity of the FSS has showed that the First Step to Success participants (children, parents, peers, and teachers) reported high levels of satisfaction with the program. Teachers using the First Step to Success in their classrooms also expressed a high degree of satisfaction with the program, remarking that it is easy to learn and relatively easy to integrate to classroom teaching procedures and has favorable results with their students (Diken & Rutherford, 1995).

It is interesting to note that the target areas in which the FSS has been shown to be effective such as aggressive behavior, on-task behavior, maladaptive behavior, and adaptive behavior are also the target areas in which children with AD/HD need intervention. However,

10

due to the lack of empirical data, it is unclear whether the FSS is equally efficacious for children with AD/HD. Additionally, the effects of the program have not been well evaluated with children with diverse cultural backgrounds.

Overall, a consensus has emerged in the past decade suggesting that the earlier intervention occurs, the more likely it is that positive outcomes will be achieved in successfully addressing at-risk children (Greenwood, 1995; Kazdin, 1987; Reid, 1993). Kazdin (1987) states that if children manifesting severe behavioral problems are not successfully intervened with the end of the third grade, then this disorder should be regarded much like a chronic disease that can be managed, but can not be cured. Indeed, follow-up studies suggest that early peer relationship problems along with academic difficulties not only indicate concurrent difficulties for the children with AD/HD, but also represent a significant "at risk" marker for later emotional and behavioral disturbance (Landau & Milich, 1990). Even those children with AD/HD who are monitored into adolescence and found to be free of psychiatric disorders appear to have some social problems, such as significantly less community and school activity involvement (Mannauzza, Klein, Bonagura, Konig, & Shenker, 1988). Nevertheless, the case for early intervention is compelling and providing intensive intervention and supports as soon as the early signs of behavior pattern are evident (Kazdin, 1987; Reid, 1993).

CHAPTER II

Review of Related Literature

This chapter begins with a discussion of the definition and prevalence of Attention Deficit/Hyperactivity Disorder, including the recent editions of the American Psychiatric Associations (APA) diagnostic manual. Research on the negative social emotional outcomes of children with AD/HD is then reviewed as clarified through clinical, epidemiological, and services research. A framework for considering the seriousness of the problem is presented. The chapter is then focused on the disruptive behaviors of children with AD/HD. Following that, emphasis is given to early prevention and intervention efforts for children with AD/HD. Finally, the chapter is concluded with a presentation of the First Step to Success program by reviewing the studies on the effectiveness of this program.

Attention Deficit/Hyperactivity Disorder

Definition

Attention deficit/hyperactivity disorder is a persistent pattern of inattention and/or hyperactivity and impulsivity that is more frequent and severe than is typically observed in individuals at a comparable level of development (DSM-IV, 1994). Core symptoms compromised of developmentally inappropriate levels of activity and impulsivity and an impaired ability to sustain attention (DSM-IV, 1994). Symptoms must be present for at least 6 months, observed before the age of 7 years, and clinically significant impairment in social, academic, or occupational functioning must be evident in more than one setting. The symptoms must not be better explained by another disorder, such as an anxiety disorder mood disorder, psychosis, or autistic disorder (DSM-IV, 1994).

DSM-IV Diagnostic Criteria

Symptoms of inattention, impulsivity, and hyperactivity are common in all children and often signify a wide range of normal developmental processes. However, when symptoms of inattention, impulsivity, and hyperactivity become excessive, this occurrence may suggest the presence of Attention-Deficit/Hyperactivity Disorder (APA, 1994). Although most individuals display symptoms of both inattention and hyperactivity-impulsivity, the Diagnostic and Statistical manual of Mental Disorder, 4th Edition (DSM-IV) distinguished between predominant ADHD symptoms patterns: 1) Inattentive Type, 2) Hyperactive-Impulsive Type, and 3) Combined Type. According to DSM-IV (American Psychiatric Association, 2000) these three subtypes are described as follows:

Attention-Deficit/Hyperactivity Disorder, Inattentive Type. This type should be used if six (or more) symptoms of inattention and six (or more) symptoms of hyperactivity-impulsivity have persisted for at least 6 months.

Attention-Deficit/Hyperactivity Disorder, Hyperactive-Impulsive Type. This subtype should be used if six (or more) symptoms of hyperactivity-impulsivity (but fewer than six symptoms of inattention) have persisted for at least 6 months. Inattention may often still be a significant feature in such cases.

Attention-Deficit/Hyperactivity Disorder, Combined Type. This subtype should be used if six (or more) symptoms of inattention and six (more) symptoms of hyperactivity-impulsivity have persisted for at least 6 months. Hyperactivity may still be used such cases, whereas other cases are more purely inattentive.

The most recent diagnostic criteria for AD/HD as defined in DSM-IV (DSM-IV, 1994) are set forth in Table 1.

Table 1

A. Either (1) or (2):

    (1) six (or more) of the following symptoms of inattention have persisted for at least 6 months to a degree that is maladaptive and inconsistent with developmental level:

        Inattention

        (a) often fails to give close attention to details or makes careless mistakes in schoolwork, work, or other activities

        (b) often has difficulty sustaining attention in tasks or play activities

        (c) often does not seem to listen when spoken to directly

        (d) often does not follow through on instructions and fails to finish schoolwork, chores, or duties in the workplace (not due to oppositional behavior or failure to understand instructions)

        (e) often has difficulty organizing tasks and activities

        (f) often avoids, dislikes, or is reluctant to engage in tasks that require sustained mental effort (such as schoolwork or homework)

        (g) often loses things necessary for tasks or activities (e.g., toys, school assignments, pencils, books, or tools)

        (h) is often easily distracted by extraneous stimuli

        (i) is often forgetful in daily activities

    (2) six (or more) of the following symptoms of hyperactivity-impulsivity have persisted for at least 6 months to a degree that is maladaptive and inconsistent with developmental level:

        Hyperactivity

        (a) often fidgets with hands or feet or squirms in seat

        (b) often leaves seat in classroom or in other situations in which remaining seated is expected

        (c) often runs about or climbs excessively in situations in which it is inappropriate (in adolescents or adults, may be limited to subjective feelings of restlessness)

        (d) often has difficulty playing or engaging in leisure activities quietly

        (e) is often "on the go" or often acts as if "driven by a motor"

        (f) often talks excessively

        Impulsivity

        (g) often blurts out answers before the questions have been completed

        (h) often has difficulty awaiting turn

        (i) often interrupts or intrudes on others (e.g., butts into conversations or games)

B. Some hyperactive-impulsive or inattentive symptoms that caused impairment were present before age 7 years.

C. Some impairment from the symptoms is present in two or more settings (e.g., at school [or work] and at home).

D. There must be clear evidence of clinically significant impairment in social, academic, or occupational functioning.

E. The symptoms do not occur exclusively during the course of a Pervasive Developmental Disorder, Schizophrenia, or other Psychotic Disorder and are not better accounted for by another mental disorder (e.g., Mood Disorder, Anxiety Disorder, Dissociative Disorder, or a Personality Disorder).

Prevalence

It is important for the practitioners to recognize that to some extent the issue of prevalence is artificially established. AD/HD is defined by observable behavior, not by a blood test or brain wave analysis. Thus, the problem is not black and white nor specifically categorical, but rather dimensional (Goldstein & Goldstein, 1998). The prevalence or incidence of AD/HD varies across studies at least in part due to different methods of selecting samples, the nature of the populations from which they are drawn (differing nationalities or ethnicities, urban vs. rural, etc.), the criteria applied to classify AD/HD (DSM criteria vs. rating scale cutoff), and certainly the age range and sex composition of the samples (Barkley, 1998). DSM-IV prevalence estimates among school children vary from 3-5%, (Keenan, Shaw, Walsh, Delliguadri, & Giovannelli, 1997; Lavigne, Gibbons, Christoffel, Arend, Rosenbaum, & Binns, 1996) but other estimates change from 1.7-16%.4, 5. However, when only the endorsement of the presence of the behavior of hyperactivity (not the clinical disorder) is required from either parent or teacher rating scales with just a cutoff on ratings, prevalence rates can run as high as 22-57%. This highlight the point that being described as inattentive or overactive by a parent or teacher does not in and of itself represent a disorder in a child (Barkley, 1998).

It is also important to note that, boys outnumber girls with a ratio of approximately 3:1 in epidemiologic surveys; the ratio is considerably higher in clinic samples. Similar figures apply to conduct disorder, which occurs in 3% to 7% of children and which demonstrates a 2:1 to 3:1 male-to-female predominance (Barkley, 1998).

15

Individuals diagnosed with AD/HD are often found to have a number of other disorders in addition to their AD/HD (Barkley, 1998). In children diagnosed with AD/HD, oppositional defiant disorder (ODD), or conduct disorder (CD) is present 25-67% of cases; 25% have co-existent anxiety disorder; 20 % have mood disorder, and 20% have specific developmental disorders, involving specific learning difficulties, language based difficulties, and motor co-ordination difficulties (Angold, Costello, & Erkanli, 1999).

According to Erald, Power, and Nezu (as cited in Angold, Costello, & Erkanli, 1999), there is already evidence that the different subtypes of AD/HD are associated with different patterns of comorbidity in particular, that emotional disorders may be more strongly associated with non-hyperactive attention deficit disorders, whereas the combined subtype is more strongly associated with CD (Erald, Power, & Nezu, 1997). Studies of clinic-referred children with AD/HD have found that between 54% and 67% will meet criteria for a diagnosis of ODD by 7 years of age or later.

In addition, comobidity has often been linked to increased levels of symptomatology within each of the disorders making up the comorbid group, and with increased levels of impairment in functioning. For instance individuals with both AD/HD and ODD or CD have higher levels of CD/ODD symptoms than children with pure CD (Hinshaw, Lahey, & Hart, 1993), greater levels of parental psychopathology, conflictual interactions with parents, peer rejection, school problems, and psychosocial adversity (Fletcher, Fisher, Barkley, and Smallish, 1996).

Although there is a consensus on the higher prevalence rates of AD/HD in the U.S., prevalence rates of AD/HD in Turkey is still a question. Most AD/HD studies conducted in Turkey investigated epidemiology and neuropsychology and very few studies explored family psychosocial characteristics and prevalence of AD/HD (Aydogdu, 2001; Ozcan, 2002). One study explored the prevalence of AD/HD and oppositional defiant disorder (ODD) in Turkish school age children and the distribution of symptoms according to subtypes (Ersan, Dogan, Dogan, & Sumer, 1994). The study population was made up of 1425 children from eight elementary schools selected by random sampling method. The study findings showed that the prevalence among the sample of Turkish children was 8. Another study investigated whether Childhood Behavior Checklist/4-18 (CBCL) and Teacher Report Form (TRF) scores of children and adolescents with a first-time diagnosis of attention-deficit hyperactivity disorder (ADHD) were different and whether there was a similar difference in typically developing control subjects (Oncu et al., 2004). The study analyzed the CBCL and TRF scores of 146 patients and the scores of 274 age and sex-matched control subjects recruited from a nationally representative sample. The findings showed that subjects with AD/HD had significantly higher CBCL and TRF scores than control subjects. Age was significantly correlated with scores on the CBCL and TRF subscales Social Withdrawal, Somatic Complaints, and Internalization Problems; with scores on the CBCL subscale Attention Problems; and with scores on the TRF subscale Anxiety–Depression. In the group of children and adolescents with AD/HD, age was negatively correlated with scores on the CBCL and TRF subscale Externalizing Problems and with scores on the TRF

17

subscale Aggressive Behavior. In the control group, the only significant correlation was between age and the CBCL subscale Somatic Complaints score. Overall, the results indicated that underdiagnosis of ADHD in childhood may cause the emergence of greater internalization problems in adolescence. The researchers interpreted that the more prominent Internalizing Problems in the adolescent group with AD/HD would be a result of social problems that these adolescent experience. The authors also pointed out that the higher somatization problems in the study sample would be a correlate of other internalization disorders and that also would reflect a cultural difference. Previous studies conducted with Turkish patients revealed that somatization is frequent in the Turkish population and may be a prominent part of depressive symptomatology (Ebert & Martus, 1994; Ulusahin, Basaoglu, & Peykel, 1994).

Erman and colleagues (2000) compared the distribution of symptoms of inattention, hyperactivity, impulsivity, and symptoms of oppositional defiant disorder (ODD) in Turkish and Canadian children, who had received a clinical diagnosis of AD/HD. 103 Canadian and 97 Turkish children, who met the DSM-IV criteria for a clinical diagnosis of ADHD were included in the study. The results showed that Turkish children were rated more hyperactive and impulsive than Canadian children by their parents. However, parent ratings did not indicate any difference in inattention.

Limited number of AD/HD studies conducted in Turkey mostly investigated epidemiology and neuropsychology and very few studies explored family psychosocial characteristics (Aydogdu, 2001; Ozcan, 2002). Existing studies of family psychosocial characteristics of children with AD/HD dealt with several aspects of families such as parent-child relationship and psychopathology of parents. Summarizing this research, it had generally been found that parents of all children at all age levels with AD/HD report deriving less comfort and value from being a parent, feeling less knowledgeable and skilled, having higher levels of stress and using more authoritarian and negative control than their counterparts whose children do not have an AD/HD (Aydogdu, 2001; Ozcan, 2002). Findings from available studies also showed that most parents tended to interpret the children as willfully defiant because their child's behavior and performance varies across activities, settings, and time (Aydogdu, 2001; Ozcan, 2002). It is important to note that when parents perceive their child's misbehavior as more the result of dispositional factors, more intentional, and more under the child's control, they are likely to express more negative effect and attribute greater importance to responding to the child's misbehavior (Dix, Ruble, Grusec, & Nixon as cited in Goldstein & Goldstein, 1998). Furthermore, the combination of negative emotional arousal in the parent and child-blaming attributions with regard to the misbehavior is linked to the increase in over reactive or harsh parenting behaviors (Smith & O'Leary, 1995).

Reviewing the educational research on AD/HD in Turkey, it is widely accepted that with the rapidly growing students with AD/HD population, Turkish teachers are being challenged as how to provide the best comprehensive educational and support services to their students with AD/HD (Ozdemir, 2006). In a study, Ozdemir (2006) explored the difference between the burnout level of teachers of students with AD/HD and teachers of non-AD/HD students in Turkey. Overall, findings revealed that there were no significant differences between the scores of teachers of students with AD/HD and teachers of non-AD/HD students. However, the Personal Accomplishment subscale score of teachers of students with AD/HD was lower than teachers of students with non-AD/HD.

The challenges in working with increasing number of students with AD/HD and their diverse families encompass many areas. The lack of culturally sensitive interventions and

19

assessment tools, the lack of written materials on the nature of the disorder and instructional strategies, and the lack of in-service training opportunities are only a few of the critical issues facing those working with students with AD/HD in Turkey. These issues are further complicated by many families who do not seek care due to the difficulties of stigma, a lack of understanding about the disorder and its' management, a lack of information about where to go for treatment, an inability to pay for care and the limited access to and availability of mental health specialists, such as psychiatrists and psychologists.

Taken as a whole, findings from studies in Turkey show the importance of attending to both parental and teacher attributions about the causes and controllability of various child behaviors in order to replace dysfunctional attributions, expectancies, or beliefs with more beneficial perspectives and practices. Thus, there is an emerging consensus that multimodal interventions involving parents, teachers, and the child himself/herself are crucial for Turkish children with AD/HD.

Family Functioning of Children with AD/HD

Consistent with the findings in Turkey, it is well documented in the literature that AD/HD is a disorder that affects a child's behavior and puts additional stress on the parent and overall family functioning. Accordingly, a recent review study in the U.S. revealed that the presence of AD/HD in children is linked to a) varying degrees with disturbances in family and marital disfunctioning, b) negative parents-child relationships, c) specific patterns of parental cognitions about child behavior and reduced parenting self-efficacy, and d) increased levels of parenting stress and parental psychopathology, especially when AD/HD is comorbid with conduct problems (Johnston & Mash, 2001).

Most researchers have indicated that the heterogeneity of AD/HD suggests multiple

20

casual pathways, with genes and environment interacting in a multitude of ways to produce the behavioral profile characteristic of the disorder (Johnston & Mash, 2001; Taylor, 1999). Given this point of view, it must be considered that at one extreme, there may be children for whom AD/HD is predominantly determined early in the development by biological risk factors, with a relatively lesser role for subsequent contributions from the family or other environmental factors (Faraone & Biederman, 1998). At another extreme, a high risk family environment may serve as the main determinant of the AD/HD symptoms, when combined with minimal child predisposition (Johnston & Mash, 2001).

From a transactional point of view, the stressful, intense, and demanding nature of the child's AD/HD features are also likely to elevate negative reactions from other family members and to exert a disruptive effect on family relationships and on psychological functioning of parents (Barkley, 1998; Johnston & Mash, 2001). Indeed, research suggests that the family environment is negatively affected by the cumulative effects of child's AD/HD, since the child with AD/HD exhibits negative social behaviors which create a greater number of negative interactions between the parent and child. These interactions are important factors in contributing to higher parent stress levels compared to those found in families with non-AD/HD children (Anastopoulos et al., 1992). Consistent with that result, a comparative study examined parenting stress with a sample of 58 children with AD/HD and 36 typically developing children and their parents. Findings of the study showed that parents of young children with AD/HD displayed greater stress and their coping skills were less adaptive than parents of non AD/HD children on the Parenting Stress Index and during the parent-child interaction observations (DuPaul, McGoey, Eckert, & VanBrakle, 2001). Similarly, another study found that mothers of preschool-age children with AD/HD reported greater amount of parenting stress than do mothers of non

21

AD/HD children (Byrne, DeWolfe, & Bawden 1998).

In summary, in the study of social emotional problems of children with AD/HD, one approach is that a child's with AD/HD's relationship with parents may serve as role models for a child's relationships with peers and others. The child may convey the psychopathology in the family relationships to his/her relationships with peers. A second approach is that family dysfunction may serve to exacerbate the child with AD/HD's symptoms whereas intense AD/HD symptoms may function as the bases of social emotional problems of children with AD/HD. Unfortunately, our understanding is limited with the existing studies that are correlational in nature and provide little insight of how associations between family factors and child problems develop over time. Certainly, there is a great need for both theoretical and empirical steps to gain a better understanding of disorder and to social behaviors of children with AD/HD.

Social Emotional Problems of Children with AD/HD

Social behavior in childhood has been shown consistently to have implications for functioning and adjustment in life. Having positive social skills has been associated with academic success, social acceptance by peers and belonging, positive self-esteem and self-confidence, morality, stress resistance, cooperative social-exchange skills, and self-control of aggressive impulses (Barkley, 1998; Stormont, 2001). On the other hand, children who have poor social relations are more likely to experience serious difficulties in later life, including truancy, antisocial behavior, social anxiety, and increased need for mental health services (Parker & Asher, 1987). Extensive research has shown that children with AD/HD have seriously disturbed social relations. More specifically, children with the disorder are less popular among their peers, and are more often rejected by their peers (Gaub & Carlson, 1997a; Hodgens, Cole, & Boldizar, 2000; Landau & Moore, 1991). Problems caused by inattention and impulse control

22

effect negatively the social performance of children with this disorder in a number of areas. First, they may enter ongoing peer activities in a sudden, disruptive manner. Second, their communication style often differs than their typically developing counterparts. Children with AD/HD have difficulty in following the implicit rules of good conversation. They are likely to interrupt others, pay minimal attention to what others are saying, and respond in an irrelevant fashion to the queries or statements of peers. Third, these children frequently approach interpersonal problems in an aggressive manner, lose their temper, and become angry quite easily. Therefore arguments and fights with peers are common (DuPaul & Stoner, 2003). Being inflexible if another child appeals, having a need to take control of play situations, becoming intimidating, and being stubborn about having things occur the way they want them to happen are other common observable behaviors of children with AD/HD (Barkley, 1998).

The social behaviors of children with attention deficit/hyperactivity disorder (AD/HD) are suggestive of underlying difficulties with emotion regulation (Melnick & Hinshaw, 2000). These children frequently exhibit increased emotionality, displaying greater degrees of explosive, unpredictable, and oppositional behavior (Mercugliano, Power, & Blum, 1999). Over reactions to minor inconveniences are common, and such children may seem overly aroused when in stimulating situations (Guevremont & Dumas, 1994). Children with the disorder have also been described as overly exuberant (Whalen & Henker, 1985), emotionally labile and inflexible to the situational demands (Landau & Milich, 1988), and intense and hyperactive (Barkley, 1997c). Likewise, peers tend to view these children as more aggressive, inflexible, intrusive, disruptive and annoying (Taylor, 1994). According to Barkley (1998), most children with AD/HD (except for those with purely inattentive symptoms) have a disinhibitory deficit, which causes secondary impairments in domains of self-regulation such as emotion.

Furthermore, Barkley (1998) emphasizes that children with the disorder display greater prepotent emotional reactivity to "charged" events and less capacity to regulate emotion/arousal states in the service of goal-directed behavior.

Although there is considerable controversy in the basic and applied literature regarding the appropriate conceptualization of emotion regulation, most researchers agree that it involves successful management of emotional arousal in a way that facilitates adaptive social functioning (Eisenberg et al., 1996). Eisenberg (2001) defines emotion regulation as "the process of initiating, maintaining, modulating, or changing the occurrence, intensity, or duration of internal feeling states, emotion-related physiological processes, and the behavioral concomitants of emotion" (p.120). In general, children's emotion regulation plays a critical role in normal social development and appears to mediate psychopathological difficulties (Casey, 1996; Cicchetti, Ackerman, & Izard, 1995). With nonclinical samples, Eisenberg and colleagues (1995, 1997) have demonstrated that children's negative emotionality and poor emotion regulation are implicated in the risk for social maladaptation. Specifically, Eisenberg et al. (2000) proposed a heuristic model in which individual differences in emotionality and regulation contribute to children's level of social competence. Children who are able to "keep cool" under emotionally arousing conditions are better able to use competent and peer-oriented solutions that yield interpersonal harmony and cooperation with rules. On the contrary, children who become overstimulated or who deal unconstructively with emotion are likely to behave aggressively, withdraw, and disrupt play (Eisenberg, Fabes, Nyman, Bernzweig, & Pinuelas, 1994).

Limited research in the area of emotion regulation in children with AD/HD has provided preliminary evidence that emotion regulation abilities are modestly related to underlying problems with impulse control and hyperactivity, and also represent a different domain of skills

24

that add incremental information to the prediction of social functioning in children with AD/HD (Melnick & Hinshaw, 2000). Developmentally inappropriate inattention and /or hyperactivity and impulsivity, posited to be central to AD/HD (Barkley, 2000), appear to overwhelm a child's capacity to self-regulate at each developmental level, thereby interfering with the development of age appropriate emotion regulation.

Melnick and Hinshaw (2000) found that impairment in emotion regulation in children with AD/HD was related to comorbid aggression rather than simply AD/HD symptomatology alone. The researchers showed that children with AD/HD in the high-aggressive groups used a less constructive pattern of emotional coping, including overresponsive emotionality and diminished problem solving, than AD/HD children in the low-aggressive groups or non-AD/HD diagnosed children. Interestingly, all children with AD/HD in this study reported more intense feelings of anger than their non-AD/HD peers when presented with emotionally arousing vignettes.

In addition, researchers have demonstrated children who are prone to intense emotion, especially negative emotion, and are low in regulation are more likely to engage in externalizing behavior associated with negative emotion (Dodge, Lochman, Harnish, Bates, & Pettit, 1997). In other words, if children experience strong negative emotions and can not sufficiently modulate their emotion and its' expression, they are more likely to behave in inappropriate ways by externalizing their negative emotions (Eisenberg, Cumberland, et al., 2001; Lemery, Essex, & Smider, 2002). Supportive of this view, researchers have shown that children with AD/HD display social behavior that is described as disruptive, controlling, trouble-making, and frequently aggressive (Melnick & Hinshaw, 1996; Pelham & Bender, 1982; Whalen & Henker, 1985). The primary features of AD/HD combined with aggression often interfere negatively with

25

an individual's ability to interact effectively with peers, family members, and others. They demand a great deal of attention from others, with their behaviors often being more intense or forceful than the situation requires (Sheridan, 1998). To make the case worse, at least one-half of all children with AD/HD are known to have comorbid problems with aggressive conduct (Hinshaw, 1987; Hodgens et al., 2000; Maedgen and Carlson, 2000). Moreover, highly aggressive AD/HD children display impairments in the social area, and are strongly rejected by their peers (Gaub & Carlson, 1997; Hinshaw & Melnick, 1995; Hodgens, Cole, & Boldizar, 2000; Landau & Moore, 1991).

In another study, Maedgen and Carlson, (2000) compared children with AD/HD combined type, children with AD/HD predominantly inattentive type (AD/HD-I), and controls on parent and teacher ratings of social status and performance, self-report of social knowledge and performance, and observations of behavior on an emotional regulation task. Their analyses indicated that children with AD/HD-C were rated as showing more aggressive behavior; furthermore, they displayed emotional dysregulation characterized by high intensity and high levels of both positive and negative behavior. In contrast, children with AD/HD-I were perceived as displaying social passivity and showed deficits in social knowledge on the self-report measure but did not evidence problems in emotional regulation.

Although children with AD/HD frequently encounter peer dislike and rejection, compelling evidence supports that these children display a "positive illusory bias" in their self-perceptions (Gresham, MacMillan, Bocian, Ward, & Forness, 1998; Hoza, Pelham, Milich, Pillow, & McBride, 1993) and overestimate their social skills when compared to same-age non-AD/HD peers (Diener & Milich, 1997). Hoza and colleagues (1993) found that children with AD/HD view themselves just as competent as comparison children in the social domain. Thus, a

26

negative sense of self was not found in children with AD/HD, despite the frequency with which these children reportedly received negative feedback and failure. Such findings show that children with AD/HD may not perceive clearly the effects of their social behaviors on their relationships with peers and overestimate their social skills. Two hypotheses were proposed for the optimism displayed by children with AD/HD regarding their social skills (Milich, 1994). The first hypothesis assumes that their sense of self may be a manifestation of cognitive immaturity. The second hypothesis suggests that the optimism may function as a self-protective mechanism, and may help them to present themselves in the best possible light (Diener & Milich, 1997). A recent study by Hoza, Pelham, Dobbs, Owens, and Pillow (2002) was conducted with the goal of reconciling the divergent findings regarding AD/HD children and self-concept. The results, as the researchers predicted, found that AD/HD boys as compared to controls tended to overestimate their scholastic competence, social acceptance, and behavioral conduct; however, it was not clear whether it was due to limited self-awareness or defensive responding. The findings indicated that the aggressive AD/HD subgroups overestimated their competence significantly more than did the nonaggressive subgroup.

From the available research, there appears to be a possible reason for the positive illusory bias that children with AD/HD exhibit in regard to their social emotional competence. It is likely that these children misjudge their level of social competence because they over-attribute hostile intention to their peers' actions thereby justifying aggressive behavior. Additionally, research supports that hostile attribution bias is strongly associated with reactive aggression. Empirical evidence suggests that children with attention problems and impulsivity tend to display reactive rather than proactive aggression (Dodge, Lochman, Harnish, Bates, & Pettit, 1997). Reactive aggression is conceptualized as emotionally driven, associated with a lack of self-control and low frustration tolerance (Berkowitz, 1989). For example, reactively aggressive children may misinterpret non-threatening social information as threatening and subsequently generate and enact responses that are defensive and aggressive (Crick & Dodge, 1996). Defensive responding may lead to a self-fulfilling prophecy whereby aggressive behavior results in additional negative peer encounters and affirmation of the hostile bias (Dodge & Pettit, 2003). In sum, emotion regulation deficits would place children with AD/HD at risk for the development of reactive aggression under emotionally arousing circumstances. Nevertheless, if children with AD/HD express more negative emotions during the early stages of a social encounter, other children may be more likely to make negative attributions about their intentions and respond accordingly. Indeed, research supports that typically developing children tend to respond to their AD/HD peers with aversion, criticism, and at times, counter aggression after only a few social contacts (Barkley, 1990).

Interestingly, extensive research shows that children with AD/HD exhibit hostile attribution bias to ambiguous interpersonal episodes. Similar self-distortions were also found in aggressive rejected children. Sandstrom and Cramer (2003) proposed that aggressive rejected children are particularly prone to engage in biased encoding processes that "protect" them from negative peer feedback. Moreover, research has described that children with aggressive behavior not only misinterpret intent but also the degree of aggressive behavior in a social situation (Dodge & Feldman, 1990; Hubbard et al., 2001). For example, when involved in an aggressive interaction, children with aggressive tendencies are more likely to underestimate their own level of aggression than are other children. These results suggest that aggressive children misjudge their level of aggression possibly because they over-attribute hostile intention to their peers' actions thereby justifying aggressive behavior.

28

Empirical evidence also suggest that hostile attribution bias is related to reactive aggression (Crick & Dodge, 1994; Dodge, Somberg, 1987) and that hostile attributions are specific to children with AD/HD who are high in aggression (Milich & Dodge, 1984). Reactive aggression has been defined as angry, impulsive and reflexive aggression, whereas proactive aggression has been defined as planned and purposeful aggression (Dodge & Coie, 1987; Vitaro, Brendgen, & Barker, 2006). Reactively aggressive children tend to display emotional difficulties, including high negative emotionality, attenuated empathy and inappropriate affective expressions (Cole, Zahn-Waxler, & Smith, 1994, Miller & Eisenberg, 1988). The degree of negative emotional behavior such as mood lability, anger dysregulation, and reactivity in a child's social milieu influences a child's social standing. It may be the case that increased levels of negativity affect both a child's perception of social cues and behavior as it may lead a child to act in an aversive manner towards peers, thus creating and/or maintaining negative social status.

It is evident that children's perception of the world and themselves impact their behavior. In this context, evaluation of the links between children's social information processing (SIP) abilities and social adjustment have lead researchers to identify a number of social cognitive deficits that partially account for emotional and behavioral disturbances (Dodge &Feldman, 1990; Dodge & Pettit, 2003). In a comprehensive review of both biological and psychological factors contributing to aggressive behavior, Dodge and Pettit (2003) noted that deficient SIP likely develops from a series of additive life events that gradually shape a child's mental representation of the world. Early harsh and negative interactions with parents and peers might result in the amplification of social cognitive difficulties. Consistent negative interactions with parents and peers, coupled with the gradual alteration of the child's environment lead to a self-fulfilling prophecy whereby emotional disturbances and aggressive behavior result from biased ocial cognitive processes and biased environmental factors (Dodge & Tomlin, 1987).

Social Skills Deficit versus Social Performance Deficit

Social skills deficits reflect knowledge deficits in the social domain. In other words,

hildren who have social skills deficits do not know appropriate social behaviors to make

riends, respond to social situations, or read social cues (Landau, Milich, & Diener, 1998;

Maedgen & Carlson, 2000). Research has shown that inattention in children may function to

lelay the acquisition of skills and reasoning related to social competence. Thus, children with

nattention may compensate for their poorer social skills or social understanding by engaging in

nore solitary or parallel play. Accordingly, by engaging in fewer interactions with peer, children

vith AD/HD may restrict their opportunities for social learning and for positive social

nteractions. As children enter school, peer interactions become more complex and involve more

ooperative and competitive interaction and less solitary or parallel play (Hartup, 1983). In this

ontext, less skilled children easily may be overlooked, resulting in social isolation and higher

evels of social problems.

In addition, Wheeler and Carlson (1994) indicated that children with AD/HD-Inattentive

ype may have deficits in both social performance and knowledge, whereas children with

AD/HD-Combined type have performance deficits. They further argued that these deficiencies

nay be differentially mediated by symptoms typically co-occurring with each subtype. Thus,

mpulsivity and hyperactivity may prevent a child with AD/HD-C from using social knowledge

ppropriately, whereas the anxiety and disorganization that characterize children with AD/HD-I

nay limit social interactions and thereby restrict acquisition of adequate social knowledge. If

uch a pattern is the nature of children with AD/HD-I, they may be too fearful to experience

ocial interactions and therefore have fewer opportunities to learn appropriate social behaviors than children with AD/HD-C.

Children who have performance deficits in the social domain also have difficulty in consistently and efficiently implementing their social skills in response to daily social challenges (Maedgen & Carlson, 2000). Children with AD/HD engage in higher rates of unmodulated behaviors that are often inappropriate in the given context and insensitive to social expectations (e.g.,yelling, running around, or talking at inappropriate times) both as verbal (teasing, commanding) and physical (hitting) (Barkley, 1998).

Social performance deficit in children with AD/HD-C is based on research findings showing that children with AD/HD interact with other people as much as their peers. Thus they have enough opportunity to learn about proper social behaviors (Wheeler & Carlson, 1994). Because these children engage in prosocial behaviors such as social initiation, that supports the fact that they do have appropriate social knowledge. Moreover, according to Dupaul and Stoner (2003) children with AD/HD-C are able to state the rules for appropriate social behavior as well as their typically developing peers. However, what makes them have problems in social situations is that they often do not act in accord with these rules. This performance deficit is consistent with the hypotheses that children with AD/HD-C are impaired in delaying responses to the environment. Thus in many social situations, they behave before they have a chance to think about the consequences of their behaviors.

Supportively, extant research has emphasized that impulsivity and hyperactivity can be the reasons that obstruct a child with AD/HD-C from displaying social knowledge properly (Maedgen & Carlson, 2000). Particularly, impulsivity may effect the social interactions of children with AD/HD negatively by causing them to act without thinking and to have a difficult time waiting their turn in games. Consequently, this behavioral style is expected to meet with dislike and subsequent peer rejection (Wheeler & Carlson, 1994).

Disruptive Classroom Behaviors

Behavioral characteristics of AD/HD are most likely to occur in the school environment where strong demands are placed on children's regulatory skills. Despite the fact that children with AD/HD form only a small minority of all students, they frequently come to the attention of their teachers because they display a high degree of externalizing behaviors (i.e., off-task behaviors that are easily observed, may distract other students, and can be disruptive to the functioning of the classroom). Presence of a child with AD/HD in the classroom has the potential to lead to an overall increase in disruptive behavior, to more time spent by the teacher on discipline, and to evoke negative reactions in typically developing peers (Whalen & Henker, 1985). In fact, because the symptoms associated with children's regulatory skills appear to be most apparent and problematic in educational settings, AD/HD has even been defined as "a school-based disorder" (Atkins & Pelham, 1991, p. 202).Consequently, children with AD/HD are also quite regularly brought to the attention of the school personnel by concerned teachers or parents, who in addition to concerns about these children's disruptive behaviors may note academic underperformance and negative social relations.

Difficulties resulting from impulsivity are often misinterpreted when children reach elementary school age since academic and social demands are increased significantly (DuPaul & Stoner, 2003). In elementary school settings, poor impulse regulation is often displayed as disruptive classroom behavior. Children with AD/HD have been rated as more off-task, disruptive, help-seeking, less able to exhibit self-control, and defiant than non-AD/HD peers (Flicek, 1992). Likewise, fidgeting, pronounced distractibility, disorganization, and impatience have been found to be often associated with AD/HD (Barkley, 1998). In addition, peers describe

32

children with AD/HD, compared with their non-AD/HD classmates, as being more noisy, as causing trouble, as getting mad when they do not get their way, as being rude to teachers, as being mean and cruel to other children, as being bossy, as bothering others, and as making fun of people (Pelham & Bender, 1982). As a result of their noncompliant, disruptive, and aggressive behaviors, children with AD/HD are rejected by their peers as early as the end of the first day of contact (Erhardt & Hinshaw, 1994) or even after one play session (Pelham & Bender, 1982).

Gender Differences in Peer Relationship Problems of Children with AD/HD

Research examining gender differences in the children with AD/HD in regard to social problems is limited. Obtaining adequate samples of girls with AD/HD to examine gender differences is particularly questionable when subjects are recruited from treatment clinics, since girls appear to be most underrepresented in referred samples. Prevalence rates vary, with male-to-female ratios in clinic-referred samples ranging from 9:1 to 6:1. Ratios for population-based studies are approximately 3:1 (DSM-IV, 1987). Very few studies have included an adequate number of female subjects to warrant gender-based comparisons of children with AD/HD. Thus, there is significantly more to be learned about how girls with AD/HD differ from boys with AD/HD in behavioral, social-emotional, and academic areas.

Among the few studies, Gaub and Carlson (1997b) quantitatively reviewed and evaluated literature examining gender differences in AD/HD providing a meta-analysis of relevant research. Domains evaluated include primary symptomatology, intellectual and academic functioning, comorbid behavior problems, social behavior, and family variables. The study indicated that there were no gender differences in social functioning, impulsivity, academic performance, fine motor skills, parental education, or parental depression. However, compared with boys with AD/HD, girls with AD/HD displayed greater intellectual impairment, lower

33

levels of hyperactivity, and lower rates of other externalizing behavior. The study also indicated that some gender differences were clearly moderated by the effects of referral source; among children with the disorder identified from nonreferred populations, girls with AD/HD showed lower levels of inattention, internalizing behavior, and peer aggression than boys with AD/HD, while girls and boys with AD/HD identified from clinic-referred samples displayed similar levels of impairment on these variables. In addition, many researchers have noted that clinic-referred samples are not representative of children with AD/HD in general, as boys usually experience higher prevalence ratios in clinic-referred samples than girls. If girls with AD/HD are less likely to be referred to clinics, it is possible that the girls referred may be the most severely affected. Therefore, studying gender differences in clinic- referred samples may lead to erroneous generalizations about girls with AD/HD (Gaub & Carlson, 1997b).

There is a significant need for future research examining gender differences in peer relationship problems of children with AD/HD with necessary attention to methodological limitations of the current literature, including the potential confounding effects of referral bias, comorbidity, and rater source. Addressing the topic of gender differences from a critical point of view will help researchers become aware of the affect of potential gender bias and give necessary attention to girls population with AD/HD. However, although gender differences in peer relationship difficulties of children with AD/HD is an important area needed to be explored, while approaching the difficulties of a child with AD/HD, it is very important to keep in mind that individual characteristics and circumstances of each child will result in unique patterns and strengths of mutual influence operating in the presentation of AD/HD syptomatology (Johnston & Mash, 2001). Studies using clinical samples have demonstrated that girls with AD/HD tend to display more severe cognitive, language, and neurological problems than boys with AD/HD. For

34

example, Berry, Shaywitz, and Shaywitz (1985) examined a group of children who were referred to the Learning Disorders Unit and Pediatric Neurology Clinic of Yale University School of Medicine for evaluation between 1979 and 1983. Their data demonstrated that girls with AD/HD showed more severe cognitive impairments than boys, especially in the area of language function. These girls were also more frequently referred for speech problems and obtained lower mean Full Scale and Verbal IQ scores. Brown, Madan-Swain, and Baldwin (1991) studied a sample of 51 boys and 20 girls with AD/HD who had been referred by pediatricians to an outpatient, university-based clinic for AD/HD. They found that girls with AD/HD were retained in school significantly more often than boys and had more impairment on spatial memory tasks. As girls with AD/HD grew older, they showed greater impairments in neurocognitive functioning and academic achievement and more peer problems than boys with AD/HD.

Aggression

Aggression has been a popular topic of study in children with AD/HD (Melnick & Hinshaw, 1996). Research has shown that children with AD/HD display social behavior that is described as disruptive, controlling, trouble-making, and frequently aggressive (Melnick & Hinshaw, 1996; Pelham & Bender, 1982; Whalen & Henker, 1985). The primary features of AD/HD combined with aggression often interfere negatively with an individual's ability to interact effectively with peers, family members, and others. Temperamental and behavioral deficits observed in young children with AD/HD interfere with typical social interactions. They demand a great deal of attention from others, with their behaviors often being more intense or forceful than the situation requires (Sheridan, 1998).

Aggression seems to be differentially linked to many factors including the type of attentional disorder (Stormont, 2001). The social outcome of aggression is associated with children with AD/HD who have both hyperactivity-impulsivity and attention problems (combined type) but not with children with AD/HD who have attention problems without excessive hyperactivity and impulsivity (Maedgen & Carlson, 2000). In particular, boys diagnosed with AD/HD-C have consistently been found to be more aggressive than boys with AD/HD-I (Lahey, Schaughency, Strauss, & Frame, 1984; Lahey et al., 1987).

Children with AD/HD with aggression frequently misinterpret neutral behaviors as hostile and confrontational, which may prompt an aggressive response (Dodge, 1993). In other words, children with AD/HD tend to make hostile attributions for ambiguous interpersonal episodes. For example, one study explored issues related to social problem solving in hyperactive-aggressive children: How and what children think under conditions of automatic and controlled processing in social problem solving situations. Children were presented with scenarios reflecting three types of everyday situations during which problems occur: Compliance with authority such as parents and teachers, interactions with peers and siblings, and persistence with academic or household tasks in a social context under two conditions: Free Association (FA) and Inquiry (I). The FA section was hypothesized to elicit automatic processing and the I section was hypothesized to elicit controlled processing of information. Findings indicated that children with AD/HD and aggression were not different in the number of solutions generated to solve a problem or to recognize the components of a problem than age-matched nonhyperactive-nonaggressive children. However they differed in proposing more aggressive solutions and were less able to anticipate consequences when compared to non-AD/HD peers (Bloomquist, Michael, August, Cohen, & Doyle, 1997). Similarly, previous research showed that aggressive children generate more qualitatively aggressive content outputs as compared to nonaggressive children (Lochman & Dodge, 1994; Mott & Krane, 1994). In addition, Hinshaw and Melnick (1995)

36

showed that aggressive children manifest fewer verbal assertation and more conflict escalation (i.e. more aggressive) solutions as compared to nonaggressive children.

It is also important to note that in various studies, children with AD/HD are rated by their peers as starting fights and arguments more than non-AD/HD children (Hodgens, Cole, and Boldizar, 2000; Maedgen & Carlson, 2000). In fact, research documented that children with AD/HD tend to be aggressive without an obvious aim except to inflict harm on a peer and are also more likely to be aggressive to obtain something valuable for them, such as to come first in a game (Atkins & Stoff, 1993).

To make the case worse, aggression is one of the most pervasive social problems for children with AD/HD (Paternite, Loney, Salisbury, & Whaley, 1999). Research showed that 67% of preschoolers at risk for AD/HD with aggression at age 3 continued to have behavior problems when they reached 9 years old (Campbell & Ewing, 1990). In addition to being predictive of future problem behaviors, research found that aggression is one of the most important behavioral predictors of peer rejection (Landau, Milich, & Diener, 1998). Indeed, children with high hyperactivity and aggression problems are more likely to display peer-rated aggression and self delinquency than their typically developing peers (Vitaro et al., 1994).

Erhardt and Hinshaw (1994) examined the influence of naturalistic social behaviors and nonbehavioral variables on the development of peer status in unfamiliar boys with AD/HD and typically developing peers. Physical attractiveness, motor competence, intelligence, and academic achievement consisted of the nonbehavioral variables whereas noncompliance, aggression, poor social actions, and isolation constituted social behaviors. From the first day, the boys with AD/HD displayed clear differences in their social behavior. The children with AD/HD were overwhelmingly rejected. The researchers concluded that social rejection of children with

37

AD/HD developed after only brief periods of peer exposure. Prosocial behavior independently predicted friendship ratings during the first week; the magnitude of the prediction, however was small. In contrast, boys' aggression or noncompliance strongly predicted negative nominations, even with nonbehavioral factors. Although the frequency of their aggressive interactions occurred only six percent of the time, this rate was twice that of non-AD/HD boys.

Childhood peer problems stand out as strong predictors of enduring social and academic difficulties (Klein & Mannuzza, 1991; Parker & Asher, 1987) and are considered among the most intervention-resistant domains of AD/HD (Hinshaw, 1992; Melnick & Hinshaw, 1996). Such children are more likely to develop conduct disorder, to participate in more delinquent or illegal acts as adolescents, and to engage in greater substance experimentation and eventual dependence and abuse than are purely hyperactive or impulsive children (Barkley, Fischer, Edelbrock, & Smallish, 1990; Biederman et al., 1996). Indeed, follow-up studies suggest that early peer problems not only indicate concurrent difficulties for the child, but also represent a significant "at risk" marker for later emotional and behavioral disturbance (Landau & Milich, 1990). Even those children with AD/HD who are monitored into adolescence and found to be free of psychiatric disorders appear to have some social problems, such as significantly less community and school activity involvement (Mannauzza, Klein, Bonagura, Konig, & Shenker, 1988). Thus, even if long-term outcome measures did not reveal subsequent adjustment problems, one is left to wonder if children with AD/HD experience the same quality of life as other children (Landau & Moore, 1991).

Overall, research suggests that the majority of children with AD/HD experience either social incompetence or aggression, or a combination of both problems. Although medications have been effective in reducing aggressive problems (Hinshaw, Henker, Whalen, Erhardt, &

38

Dunnington, 1989), it does not increase positive behavior nor does it normalize the peer status of AD/HD children (Landau & Moore, 1991; Whalen et al., 1989). Thus, despite the popularity of pharmacotherapy, a psychosocial intervention is necessary to enhance children with AD/HD's social functioning with peers and adults (Whalen & Henker, 1991).

Given protracted nature of the disorder and the attendant long term risks for a large percentage of children with AD/HD, there is an emerging consensus that effective psychosocial interventions are critical for children with AD/HD. Following section provides an overview of the various interventions that have been supported as beneficial for children with AD/HD.

Psychosocial Interventions

Interventions for children with AD/HD and disruptive behaviors often include parent management training and behavioral intervention along with social skills training. Various training programs exist but all strive to promote more positive, compliant, and generally prosocial behavior while decreasing negative, defiant, and disruptive behavior in children (Shelton et al., 2000). These programs generally focus on peer relations, classroom conduct, and school achievement (Arnold et al., 1997; Bierman, Miller, & Stabb, 1987).

One of the most widely used psychosocial interventions that directly targets peer relationships is social skills training (SST). Social skills training was developed for the purpose of enhancing the peer relationships of rejected and neglected children. It is based on the social skills deficit model, which posits that a child's lack of social skills results in less positive peer interactions and lower social status.

Although short-term effects of SST are positive, long-term outcomes reveal discouraging results on social, vocational, and academic measures (Carlson & Bunner, 1993; Charles & Schain, 1981). Apparently, the nature of AD/HD requires certain changes in both the content and he form of the interventions (Mrug, Hoza, & Gerdes, 2001). In particular, research shows that children with AD/HD-C display performance deficit rather than a skill deficit. In other words, children with AD/HD are able to express the socially appropriate rules and behaviors, but they often do not act accord with these rules (DuPaul, 2003). Social performance deficits are more complicated to ameliorate than social skills deficits for two reasons. First, existing social relationship interventions focus on deficits in skills rather than deficits in performance. Furthermore, because social performance problems exist across settings (e.g., classroom, playground, neighborhood), interventions addressing these difficulties must be carried out by various individuals in a cross-situational fashion (DuPaul, 2003).

The other main problem is that most SST programs are designed for children who are apparently rejected without considering the unique topography of each child's performance in the social domain. In other words, pretreatment assessment data may not have been gathered to clarify the specific needs of each treated child, thus leading to a poor fit between presenting problems and SST objectives (Landau, & Milich, 1998). Obviously, children with AD/HD-I who are withdrawn and isolated are different than children with AD/HD-C who display hyperactive and impulsive symptoms (Wheeler & Carlson, 1994). Thus, a social skills deficit approach may be applied to the children with AD/HD-I whereas performance deficit approach may work with children with AD/HD-C.

Another important area to review is related to the structure of social skills interventions. Social knowledge and the acquisition of prosocial behaviors are thought and practiced generally in group therapy formats. However, research indicates that traditional group therapy format do not lead to stable changes in social relationships of children with AD/HD in "real-world" environments (DuPaul & Stoner, 2003). The lack of maintenance and generalization of social skills training become a major problem because of the fact that appropriate social behaviors are not essentially prompted by adults and peers on a consistent basis (DuPaul & Stoner, 2003). Thus, the generalization of the newly acquired skills to other contexts requires their reinforcement across different settings in the child's natural environment for an enough period of time (Mrug, Hoza, & Gerdes, 2001). Essential components of environmental programming may involve teaching parents and teachers to reinforce children to perform the behaviors trained in the social skills sessions and developing contingency management programs at home and at school to prompt trained skills (DuPaul & Eckert, 1994). Therefore, it is critical to accomplish the inclusion of teachers and parents as crucial members of the "social skills treatment team" for generalization.

A considerable problem is that once the child is rejected, peers cognitive processing of the child behavior becomes biased. In other words, the peers may develop a negative stereotypical perspective of the child, and as a result of their view, the peers may selectively perceive and respond to the stereotype-consistent behaviors (Mrug, Hoza, & Gerdes, 2001). Thus, social skills interventions not only should work on changing the negative social behaviors of children with AD/HD, but also the interventions should attempt to increase peers awareness of positive changes in children behaviors (Mrug, Hoza, & Gerdes, 2001). In order to do that, peers should be allowed to play active roles in every phases of social skills intervention. Specifically peers can participate in the social skills training sessions as role models and encourage the enactment of positive social behaviors of children with AD/HD (DuPaul, 2003). Indeed, research supports that including diverse peer group rather than using only children with disturbed behaviors increases the success of social skills training (Ang & Hughes, 2002).

Further, individuals within the child's natural environment such as parents typically have not been involved in training. Thus providing parents with necessary knowledge and training not only increases the continuity of the program but also, the intensity. Indeed, parents are generally with their children more than are teachers; this puts parents in the top position to create difficult behavior environments, or, more constructively, to provide long term interventions. Parents who are educated in the description, causes, prognosis, and treatment of AD/HD are better able to facilitate behavioral change in their children (DuPaul, Guevremont, & Barkley, 1991). Likewise, interventions can be more effective especially with respect to generalization of improved behavior across settings, when parental involvement is combined with social skills training programs.

In addition, family characteristics and secondary symptoms with regard to family functioning, such as aggressive behavior, have been shown to be among the most significant predictors of long-term negative outcome for children with AD/HD (Weiss & Hechtman, 1986). According to Doberman (as cited in Goldstein & Goldstein, 1998), positive future outcome for all children has been associated with stable family environments, consistent discipline, positive parental expectations for their future, positive parents-child relationships, perceptions of competence perceived by parents, and low rates of parental criticism. Behavioral treatment that teaches parents to modify their reactions to the child's primary symptoms, should directly alter parental negative responses, and also train parents to increase their positive responses to children (Wells et al., 2000). However, the use of their relationship as a positive corrective experience in changing the relationship patterns of the child requires insight and support over time. Family members should learn skills to apply behavioral interventions in a supportive environment and gain knowledge to identify indicators of emerging negative manifestations that will need assessment and intervention modifications (Barkley, 1998). Observing the child/parent

42

interaction and then coaching parents in providing corrective behavioral interventions can be used via home visits while utilizing an empathic approach to the child and parents.

Finally inclusion of parents in the SST program establishes consistency between the school and home environments. There must be a continuity of behavioral expectations between home and school. Discussing behavioral strategies, rewards, and limits with parents to ensure continuity of approach to dealing with challenging behaviors between home and school is crucial. In that way, parents can encourage the same skills and performance at home and in different peer groups. Indeed many children with AD/HD appear to need very strong and intense levels of reinforcement to produce appropriate behavior in certain settings (Barkley, 1997b; Landau & Moore, 1991). Parents must learn to identify the specific behaviors they want to substitute and then by giving rewards for the new more appropriate behavior, teach the child how to control his actions and reactions. This is particularly important for children who have difficulty with anger management. An anger management program focused on adaptive ways of managing anger in children with AD/HD and a behavioral skills training program focused on both social skills and motivation can be used to help children with AD/HD experience more positive social outcomes.

Another most widely used form of psychosocial interventions for young children is parent management training. Parent management training aims to alter parental disciplinary practices, including reducing the frequency of coercive exchanges between parents and children. In addition, parents are encouraged to consistently monitor their children to prevent antisocial behavior (e.g., physical aggression) and to prevent accidental injuries associated with impulsive behavior (DuPaul & Stoner, 2003).

Despite the success of training programs for parents of children with AD/HD, improvements in child behavior within the family do not significantly transfer to school or to other environments (Anastapoluos, Barkley, & Shelton, 1996). Anastopoulos and colleagues (1996) posit such programs work because they lower parental stress by teaching them to regard disruptive behaviors as less severe than previously thought. The teaching of skills to ignore minor missteps is a common element in parental training programs (Barkley, 1997b). Furthermore, parent training only treats one of the many environments of which a child is a part. In fact, research indicates that the key to change is connecting conduct at home with conduct at school while creating a system of communication between the two (Goldstein & Goldstein, 1998).

Results of such psychosocial interventions, at least in the short term, have been promising, but evaluations of the longer-term effects of these programs are quite limited at the moment (Shelton et al., 2000). Conversely, prospective studies of children with AD/HD provide the best opportunity to understand more thoroughly the adult outcomes of AD/HD. Because of the heavy burden of suffering of AD/HD and the short-term effectiveness of the interventions, there is a compelling argument in favor of an increased emphasis on primary prevention efforts. However, until recently, minimal research has been conducted to aid practitioners in identifying and supporting young children at risk for this disorder.

In a recent review study from Center for Evidence-Based Practice: Young Children with Challenging Behavior, Joseph and Strain (2003) reviewed eight comprehensive, evidence-based social emotional preventive curriculum for young children with challenging behaviors. Researchers gave each curricula an estimated degree of confidence based on nine confidence criteria. A high confidence rating was given if the literature provided evidence for seven or more of the following adoption criteria: (a) treatment fidelity, (b) treatment generalization, (c) treatment maintenance, (d) social validity of outcomes, (e) acceptability of interventions, (f) replication across investigators, (g) replication across clinical groups, (h) evidence across ethnic/ racially diverse groups, and (i) evidence for replication across settings. Among the eight successful social-emotional curricula in promotion of interpersonal skills and the reduction or prevention of challenging behavior for a wide range of children, the First Step to Success Early Intervention Program was one of two programs rated as high-confident programs.

In another review of school-based aggression prevention programs for young children, Leff, Power, Manz, Costigan, and Nabors (2001) has critically reviewed literature in an effort to identify best practices in aggression prevention programming. 34 programs were evaluated on the following standards established by Chambless and Hollon (as cited in Leff, Power, Manz, Costigan, & Nabors, 2001): (a) an experimental group design including the use of random assignment procedures;·(b) a well-documented treatment procedure; (c) uniform therapist training and treatment integrity monitoring procedures; (d) multimethod outcome measures demonstrating adequate reliability and validity; (e) assessment of effects at follow-up (at least 6-month follow-up); and (f) replication conducted by different investigators. Only five programs were met all of the above criteria except for an independent replication and referred to as "possibly efficacious". These programs were Promoting Alternative Thinking Strategies (PATHS), Second Step, the First Step to Success program, Anger Coping program, and Brain Power program. This study emphasized that the First Step to Success program provided strong empirical support for the maintenance of certain treatment gains several years following treatment and information documenting that their intervention was viewed as important, acceptable, and feasible, though costly and somewhat intensive.

In the next section, since the detailed information about the First Step to Success early intervention program is presented in the Chapter III, the Method Section, an overview of the program and extensive information in regard to the studies that demonstrated the effectiveness and social validity of the program will be provided.

The First Step to Success (FSS) Early Intervention Program

The First Step to Success (FSS) is an early intervention program developed specifically for kindergartners who indicate clear signs of developing an antisocial behavior pattern. The First Step to Success includes three components: a kindergarten-wide screening process, the classroom-based CLASS curriculum, and HomeBase, which incorporates the use of a trained consultant to work with children, teachers, and parents. The FSS is a collaborative home and school intervention program that recruits parents as partners with the school in teaching the at-risk young children about choices and consequences and a behavior pattern contributing to school success and the development of friendships. This early intervention program is designed to achieve secondary prevention goals.

Effectiveness and Social Validity of the First Step to Success Program

Research exists documenting the efficacy and social validity of the First Step to Success program for children display disruptive behavior since 1998 (Golly, Sprague, Walker, Beard, & Gorham, 2000; Perkins-Rowe, 2001; Overton, McKenzie, King, & Osborne, 2002; Walker, Kavanagh, Stiller, Golly, Severson, & Feil, 1998). Recent investigations have established that the program results in decreases in aggressive and disruptive behaviors as reported by the teacher, and increases in teacher ratings of adaptive behavior and classroom observations of on-task behavior (Walker et al., 1998). Findings indicated that the program is equally efficacious for boys and girls. In addition, observations confirmed that treatment effects

46

were largely maintained over a 2 year period (Walker et al., 1998).

In the initial evaluation study of the First Step to Success program, Walker and colleagues (1998) carried out an experimental design using a wait-list control group and randomly assigning children to groups. The program was implemented and evaluated over a 2-year period with a total of 46 kindergartners, who met study participation criteria and identified as being at risk for developing serious antisocial behavior patterns. Of the at-risk kindergartners exposed to the program, 26% of the participants were female, 33% were already receiving additional school services, 7% were of minority status, 37% lived in families with low income, and 11% screened as eligible for special education services. Over a three-month period, all study participants received the First Step to Success program. Dependent measures used to evaluate children's outcomes consisted of four teacher rating measures, including Child Behavior Checklist-Aggression subscale, and an observational measure of Academic Engagement Time (AET). The results indicated that four of the five dependent measures were sensitive to the intervention and showed a causal relationship between behavior differences and exposure to the intervention, beyond the effect of initial baseline scores. On the contrary, only teacher ratings of withdrawn behavior did not change as a function of the intervention. The effect sizes averaged .86 and ranged from .26 and 1.17 across the five dependent measures. Furthermore, 18 Cohort 1 participants were followed up into second grades, and 15 Cohort 2 subjects were followed up only into Grade 1. The effects of the First Step to Success program demonstrated significant durable effect across diverse school years, classroom settings, teachers, and peer groups for Cohort 1 and 2 participants.

The initial findings on the First Step to Success program were successfully replicated by the same research team in another investigation (Golly et al., 1998). Golly, Stiller, and Walker

1998) conducted two critical studies in order to replicate the effectiveness of the First Step to Success program with a new group of at-risk kindergartners and evaluate the social validation of the program by implementers and consumers. The findings of study one showed that substantial gains were achieved on four of the five dependent measures from pre- to postintervention time points. In contrast, the social withdrawal measure of the Teacher Report Form (TRF) of the CBCL was not sensitive to the First Step to Success program. These findings are similar in level and direction to those obtained in the original field test of the First Step intervention (Walker et al., 1998). As in the original study, 4 measures of the CBCL demonstrated very similar levels of postintervention gain for participants in the field test and replication samples. The large effect sizes obtained for 4 measures indicated strong efficacy for the intervention. In terms of social validity results, study 2 explored the social validity of the program in three areas: (1) consumer satisfaction with inservice training procedures applied to teach the minimum skills required to effectively carry out the intervention (2) follow-up of workshop participants to clarify the number that actually implemented the intervention, the number of those who did not, and the reasons why; and (3) the intervention components and outcomes that implementing participants considered to be either of critical importance or objectionable. Evaluation responses showed that educators who participated in workshops rated the content and quality of the training highly. Specifically 43 educators who implemented the intervention reflected that (1) it was effective in teaching appropriate behavior, (2) it had a positive effect on the target child's peer relations, and (3) it was relatively easy to use and manage as part of general teaching duties. On the contrary, some educators found the program as being costly, intensive, and most appropriate for children with extremely serious behavior problems (Golly, 1998).

Perkins-Rowe (2001) implemented the First Step to Success program with a multiple-baseline across subjects and settings design study in order to evaluate the direct effects of the First Step to Success on the behaviors of targeted kindergarten children who showed early signs of developing antisocial behaviors, and the collateral effects of this intervention on the behaviors of peers, the teacher, and the overall classroom environment. The findings indicated that the academic engagement behaviors of participant children increased after completing the program, while student problem behaviors decreased. In addition, improvements on teacher ratings of behavior and the classroom ecology, class wide academic engaged time, and the percent of positive social interactions were confirmed once more with this study findings.

Overton, McKenzie, King, and Osborne (2002) carried out the First Step to Success program with 22 kindergartners (aged 5-6 yrs) identified as being at risk for developing serious antisocial behavior patterns. The study showed that16 children who completed the program demonstrated significant but variable behavioral gain measured by the Child Behavior Checklist (CBCL). The children also increased the amount of time they were academically engaged (AET) an average of 28%. Their teachers and families in general reported satisfaction with the children's behavioral and academic improvement.

In a recent study, Diken & Rurherford (2005) implemented the First Step to Success program with Native American children at risk for antisocial behavior problems to examine (1) the effectiveness of the First Step to Success (FSS) program, and (2) possible cultural barriers to success of the program. Targeted children's nonsocial and social play behaviors, targeted children's problem behaviors, class-wide student behaviors, and teacher behaviors were explored for the first purpose of the study. The perceptions of participant teachers and parents regarding the First Step to Success program were also addressed for the second purpose of the study. The findings from observations showed that all participant children's social play behaviors

49

significantly improved while their nonsocial behaviors relatively decreased as soon as the intervention initiated. Teacher ratings also demonstrated significant decreases on especially CD (Conduct Disorder) behaviors and AP (Attention Problems) behaviors. In contrast, some teachers did not report positive changes either on targeted children's play behaviors or problem behaviors. Overall, most participant teachers found the FSS program effective while some found it somewhat effective in increasing target child's positive behavior. The teachers also reported that the First Step to Success program helped them to have a more positive teaching approach, and more positive interactions with all students in the class. In addition, the parents generally reported significant decreases on targeted children' problem behaviors. In terms of potential cultural barrier to effectiveness of the program, it was reported by a participant teacher that parental views of education or schooling of some Native-Americans combined with additional risk factors such as low socio-economic level and substance abuse might be a cultural barrier in the implementation of the First Step to Success program.

Overall, the First Step to Success program is an intensive classroom and home-based early identification and intervention program that was developed for at-risk kindergartners who show the early signs of an antisocial behavior pattern. Despite its promise as an effective prevention program, more research remains to be conducted with children with diverse cultural backgrounds and studies in different contexts, such as playgrounds, lunchrooms, and hallways. In addition, the First Step to Success program is an adaptation and extension of Hops and Walker's (1998) well-validated CLASS program for conduct-disordered children. In a review study on social skills problems of children with AD/HD, Landau and Milich (1998) pointed out that the CLASS program may produce significant gains for children with AD/HD, although empirical support for this assertion has not been established. Considering this assertion and

50

effectiveness of the First Step to Success program, the present study will further examine the effectiveness of the program with Turkish children with AD/HD.

CHAPTER III

The Method

Setting

The School

This study was carried out in Sincan school district, Ankara, the capital city of Turkey. Sincan is a suburban county which is one of least developed areas in Ankara. Sincan school district was selected for this study for two reasons: (1) Most families who lived in Sincan were middle or low income families with children, and (2) Research and Guidance center in Sincan school district made increasing number of student referrals to child mental health clinics for the assessment of children who displayed symptoms related to AD/HD. Thus, Sincan school district provided a large student population that was composed of students who had been clinically diagnosed with AD/HD and who could be eligible for the study criteria.

As a legal procedure, students in general education classes who have academic and behavioral difficulties are referred to RGC by their teachers for educational assessment. RGC serves as a child study laboratory to determine if a further psychological assessment is needed for a child and if an alternative educational setting is necessary. Thus, each district's RGC has a database of schools that have students with AD/HD

The Classrooms

This study was carried out in four first grade classrooms. First grade classrooms held half-day classes with approximately 43 students in each classroom. First grade classes started at 8 a.m. and ended at 12:30 pm. Students had 6 classes and each class lasted for 40 minutes. There were also 5 breaks between classes and each break lasted for 10 minutes. The daily lessons of classrooms were intended to teach students reading, writing, math, art, and physical education.

Participants

A total of 4 participant children, their teachers, and parents participated in this research. Participant children, teachers and parents met with the following criteria: The children must (1) be enrolled in a kindergarten or first grade classroom, (2) be 5-8 years old (3) be clinically diagnosed with AD/HD or clinically identified as at risk for AD/HD (4) display evidence of aggressive behavior pattern as identified by the SRSS, and (6) provide consent to participate in the research (both parent consent and child assent). The parent(s) of participant children must (1) be the closest caregivers of participant children, (2) not receiving any counseling or family-based intervention for the last two years, and (3) provide consent to participate in the research. Teachers must (1) teach in the participant children' classrooms, (2) provide consent to participate in the research.

Participant Children

Two groups of Turkish children were participated in this study. Each group (Groups 1 and Groups 2) included two first graders. All participant children were 7-year- old males who had been clinically diagnosed with AD/HD prior to the study. Children were attending regular first grade classrooms without receiving any special education services at the time of the study.

Participant children were identified by their teachers as at-risk for antisocial behaviors by using the *Student Risk Screening Scale-SRSS* (Drummond, Eddy, Reid, & Bank, 1994) before the implementation of the FSS program. Among the 7 classrooms, (4 first grade and 3 kindergarten) only four classrooms had 4 study candidates who received 15 or higher scores from the SRSS and who had been clinically diagnosed with AD/HD.

52

The third of four screening options offered in the First Step to Success Implementation Guide, the SRSS was chosen because it has better predictive ability than the first two options listed, and takes less time to use than the fourth option, which also requires parental consent (Walker et al., 1997). The SRSS checklist asks the teacher to rate all students in the class on seven behavior categories on a scale of 0 to 3: steal; lie, cheat, sneak; behavior problem; peer rejection; low achievement; negative attitude; and aggressive behavior. The checklist was translated into Turkish by the researcher and was peer reviewed for language accuracy.

Student 1, Mert.

Mert was a 7-year-old-boy who had been recently diagnosed with AD/HD. He enjoyed coming to school everyday. He eagerly participated in all games and gross motor play. He loved soccer so much and wanted to be a professional soccer player when he grows up. He also loved his younger siblings and enjoyed playing with them too.

According to his classroom teacher, Mert was frequently aggressive, was often non-compliant with requests, had great difficulty sitting still, talked excessively, and had marked difficulty completing his schoolwork. His teacher reported no fewer than 3 episodes of hitting other kids every day. Mert had received a score of 16 on the SRSS screening and became eligible to join the study.

Mert had three younger siblings and lived at an apartment with his middle income family. Mert's mother is a homemaker, and his father works at a local store as an electrical technician. According to her mother, she was responsible for most of his discipline and helping him with schoolwork. No family history of mental illness was reported, although Mert's mother reported a great deal of anxiety because of some family problems between her husband's mother and herself.

Mert's mother reported extreme concerns about her son's behavior and expressed her fear that she was unable to handle him. She reported responding in a punitive manner to Mert's misbehavior. The madder she felt, the more punitive she became. She stated that her disciplinary tactics, which included numerous spankings, had no effect on Mert.

Student 2, Oguz.

Oguz was a 7-year-old boy who had been recently diagnosed with AD/HD attending a first grade regular education classroom. He was an adorable boy with a lively personality. Oguz was blessed with a natural artistic talent and he fascinated others with his wonderful paintings. He had a great sense of humor and was able to cope and work through his problems with humor. He liked fishing, bicycling, swimming, and a variety of cartoons.

His teacher recommended Oguz because his off-task behavior was disruptive for the entire class. According to his teacher, Oguz was out of his seat a lot, didn't listen, and was disruptive and immature. He also talked when the teacher talked and required one-on-one attention in order to complete tasks. He frequently pushed in line and blamed others when the teacher corrected him. His teacher was frustrated by the amount of effort it took to correct his behavior. Oguz had received a score of 15 on the SRSS screening.

Oguz appeared accustomed to having the teacher's attention. He was frequently out of his seat to get the teacher's attention and get her feedback on his work. As soon as she gave approval, he sat back down, made a few quick marks on his paper, and then went looking for her again. His teacher emphasized that Oguz was a very smart boy and he learned reading very early. However, since her class included a large number of children with high needs (a total of 41 students), it was almost impossible for her to provide Oguz with the individual attention he needed.

Oguz's parents were well-educated and had attended college. His mother was working as a clerk for government and his father was working as an accountant. Both parents expressed that Oguz was a very smart and happy child at home. However they were concerned that Oguz was often bored at school. Both parents stated that Oguz did not want to go to school anymore, as his teacher did not offer him anything on his level. They were thinking about changing his school however since they plan to buy a new home and need to save money for the home, they had to stay close to Oguz's grandmother for a while who was responsible for taking care of Oguz.

Student 3, Selim.

Selim was a 7-year-old boy who had been recently diagnosed with AD/HD and ODD. A handsome smile and urge for excitement is a great way to describe Selim. He enjoyed outdoor play and soccer with friends. Selim said when he grows up he wants to be a football player and if that does not work out, he will look at other options.

According to his teacher, Selim was very aggressive, hitting and pushing his peers, and did not have any interest in school work. His teacher had explained major concerns in the areas of stealing, lying, poor anger control, noncompliance, and hitting and fighting with peers. She also underlined that Selim's peers didn't like him. He was frequently in trouble, and was suspended on one occasion for pushing another student. Selim had couple of older friends at school who also have significant behavior problems. His teacher was extremely concerned that Selim's older friends were engaged in stealing from people who travel using a local train and Selim would end up joining them if he does not get necessary help for his problems. Selim had received a score of 19 on the SRSS screening and became eligible to the join the study

Selim's teacher also explained that when she tried to talk to Selim's family about his problems with stealing, his family got mad at her and told her that they are a very religious

55

family, and because of that reason none of their children could do such a bad behavior. Selim's teacher said that she had no contact with the family after that discussion.

Selim was from a large family who recently moved to Ankara from a rural small town in Eastern part of Turkey. He was the third of the 8 children with a little income. His family was struggling with multiple issues, including financial problems, health problems, and adjusting to the city life. Selim's mother said that she had a hard time getting Selim to comply at home. His mother complained that she had to tell him over and over to do something at home. She got mad and wound up yelling or sometimes hitting at him.

Student 4, Serhat.

Serhat was a 7-year-old boy who had been recently diagnosed with AD/HD. He was a cheerful, active and happy child who enjoyed watching cartoons, playing sports and games that involved running, jumping or any other physical activity. Drawing, coloring and being around other children were also some of his other favorite activities.

His teacher had observed problems with physical aggression, being out of his seat a lot, not following teacher directions, frequent complaints of illness, and peer rejection. Serhat didn't listen, and was disruptive and immature. According to his teacher, he kept turning around and talking to his friends behind him, and made faces and acted silly on a routine bases. His teacher tried to ignore minor negative behaviors but after a while they would build up and she would reprimand Serhat. His teacher was concerned about Serhat's disruptive and aggressive behavior in the classroom and on the playground and was worried of what would happen to him without intervention. Serhat had received a score of 17 on the SRSS screening.

Serhat's mother was a homemaker and his father was a police officer. Her mother was also concerned about Serhat's aggressiveness, and explosive behavior at home. According to her,

Serhat was jealous of his older sister a lot and wanted all the attention on himself. She also explained that when she tries to help her daughter, such as on a school work, Serhat would act out in an extreme way and does not let her to do anything individually with her daughter. In her words, since they were living with her mother-in- law and father-in-law, disciplining her son was very difficult. She thought that Serhat's grandmother and grandfather spoiled Serhat by giving him everything he wants and making him very powerful at home.

Participant Teachers

A total of 10 Turkish teachers were contacted and informed about the study (three kindergarten, four first grade, and three second grade). All contacted teachers nominated their students on the SRSS. Of all teachers, four first grade teachers indicated that they had students who show clear sings of antisocial behavior pattern and who also had been clinically diagnosed with AD/HD. All teachers were female between the ages of 24 and 32. All teachers had college degrees and held teacher certification. In addition, teachers' years of experience ranged from 3 to 8 years.

Participant Parents

Teachers of candidate children for the FSS program arranged a meeting with parents of the eligible children for the FSS program. All eligible children's mothers attended to a first meeting along with the children's teachers. To elicit cooperation from parents to help their child be more successful at school, the researcher first introduced herself and welcomed parents. After commenting positive characteristics of their child, the researcher talked about adjustment from home to school and what we need to teach to help the child to be more successful at school. The researcher then overviewed the FSS program with parents and explained the parents the purpose of the FSS program and her study. Finally the researcher asked the parents for their cooperation. All parents voluntarily agreed be participants of the study and gave consent to the researcher.

The researcher gathered some general information from the parents after gathering their consent to join the study. Specifically, the researcher asked the parents for their ages, number of children in their household, their SES, when and by whom their children's diagnosed with AD/HD, the type of AD/HD that their children had and whether they were planning to join another special intervention or treatment program during the time of the study or not? All Turkish participating parents ranged in ages from 27 to 44. In regard to education level of parents; one mother did not go to school, one mother had secondary school degree, and two mothers had college degrees. In addition, one father had elementary school degree, one father had high school degree, and two fathers had college degrees. Parent 1, had middle level, Parents 2 and 4 had upper middle level, and Parent 4 had income levels.

Independent Variable

The independent variable in the First Step program is an early intervention program that is designed specifically for young children who indicate clear signs of developing an antisocial behavior pattern. It is a joint home and school intervention that assists at-risk young children make the best start possible in school by teaching them to get along with teachers and peers, and to engage in schoolwork. The First Step to Success enhances early school experiences by enlisting the coordinated support and participation of the three social agents who are most significant in their lives: Parents, teachers, and peers. The program has three components: First Step screening, CLASS, and HomeBase, which will be briefly discussed below.

The First Step Screening

The First Step Screening is designed to evaluate each child equally for antisocial behavior pattern and to identify those with an elevated risk for developing an antisocial behavior pattern. There are four options for achieving the screening-identification tasks for the program. In the first option the teacher is asked to nominate children whose characteristics behavior pattern reflect antisocial behavior. In the second option, the teacher rates the highest ranked children on a nine-item scale that identifies children having higher than normal rates of aggressive behavior. In the third option (SRSS), the teacher is asked rate all students in the class on seven behavior categories on a scale of 0 to 3: steal, lie, cheat, sneak; behavior problem, peer rejection, low achievement, negative attitude, and aggressive behavior. In the final option, a multiple-gating procedure which includes three interrelated stages of screening is used. This procedure consists of (1) teacher nomination and rank-ordering; (2) teacher and parent ratings; and (3) direct observations in classroom and free-play settings.

The First Step School Intervention: CLASS

The CLASS (Contingencies for Learning Academic and Social Skills) program is adapted from the well-validated school version of CLASS Program for acting out children developed by Hops and Walker (1988). The CLASS addresses symptomatology commonly associated with hyperactivity, such as oppositional, disruptive, and aggressive behaviors that typically occur in school settings (Hops & Walker, 1988).The implementation of the program requires 30 school days. Each day, the target child is given clear performance criterion that must be met before proceeding to the next day program and rewarded and praised for successfully meeting increasingly demanding expectations. The CLASS is divided into three phases: the consultant phase, the teacher phase, and maintenance.

Consultant Phase.

During the consultant phase (days 1-5), the consultant coordinates the entire

59

implementation process, and runs the program. The consultant implements the program in the classroom for two sessions, beginning with 20 minutes and progressing to 30 minutes by the time the teacher phase begins (one in the morning one in the afternoon). The consultant sits by the target child's desk, monitors the child's classroom behavior and provides feedback on the appropriateness of the child's behavior. In order to administer this feedback, the consultant randomly selects a 30-second interval and awards points for appropriate behavior and give feedback to the child with a card that is green on one side (for "GO" behaviors) and red on the other side (for "STOP" behaviors). If the child meets this criterion at 80% of time, the entire class receives a reward and the target child receives a home-based reward as well. In this phase, the consultant shows the program to the teacher and trains the teacher in how to apply it.

Teacher Phase.

The teacher implements the program daily during Program Days 6 through 20 with support from the consultant. The teacher awards the target child with points and praise every 5 minutes on Day 6. The length of time between point opportunities increases as the length of the program sessions increases from 20 to 30 minutes. The teacher starts using the card to show the child whether he is doing what is expected by turning it to green side, or remind him to stop by showing the red. In this phase, the teacher works closely with consultant, child, and parents and is also responsible for communicating with parents about the child's daily school performance.

Maintenance Phase.

The maintenance phase includes Program Days 21 through 30. The teacher continues to implement the program in this final phase. The child's appropriate behavior is maintained primarily via social praise at school and via more tangible awards at home. The use of the card is finished and feedback frequency is reduced. If the child's behavior regresses "booster" sessions can be used with the Implementation Guide directions until appropriate behavior is again established.

HomeBase

The family-based component of the First Step to Success program aims to promote school success by recruiting parents as partners in the program. The HomeBase starts from the program day 11 and takes six weeks to be completed. Each week the program consultant provides parents with interrelated lessons and teaches parents key skills for supporting and improving their child's school adjustment and performance via home visits. The consultant also provides support and assistance to parents so that parents may apply program skills correctly and consistently. The skills discussed each week include: communicating and sharing school, cooperation, setting limits, solving problems, making friends, building confidence. The parents then do the skill-building activities with the child for 10 to 15 minutes each day.

Dependent Variables and Measures

To adequately address the research questions of the study, four dependent variables were measured and interviews were conducted with participant teachers and parents in the study. The four dependent variables consist of: (1) children's social-emotional problems (2) children's problem behaviors; (3) class-wide student behaviors; and (4) teacher behaviors.

Participant children's social emotional problems were examined with;

(a) teacher and parent ratings of the Turkish version the Child Behavior Checklist (CBCL-TRF).

Participant children's problem behaviors were examined with;

(a) teacher ratings of the Turkish version of the AD/HD Rating Scale-IV

(b) observations of academic engagement behaviors

Class-wide teacher behaviors and student behaviors were evaluated with;

(a) teacher ratings of changes in teachers' behaviors and class-wide student behaviors via the Turkish version of the Teacher Ratings of Behavior.

A description of all dependent variables and measures is presented in Table 2.

Table 2

Dependent Variables and Measures

Dependent variables & measures	Target population	Frequency &When
Social Emotional Problems (Question 1)		
1. Child Behavior Checklist (CBCL) (Achenbach, 1991)	Targeted children	[Three times]
2. Teacher Report From (TRF)	Targeted children	Pre, Post, and Follow-up
Problem Behaviors (Question 2)		
3. ADHD Rating Scale-IV	Targeted children	[Three times]
4. Observational data	Targeted children	Pre, Post, and Follow-up
Class-wide student behaviors (Question 3)	Whole class	[Twice]
5. Teacher Ratings of Behavior (Perkins-Rowe, 2001)	Teachers	Pre-and- Post-intervention
Teacher behaviors (Question 4)		[Twice]
6. Teacher Ratings of Behavior (Perkins-Rowe, 2001)	Teachers	Pre- and Post-intervention

In addition, interviews with participant teachers and parents were conducted in order to provide insight into participant teachers' and parents' opinions of the feasibility and effectiveness of the First Step to Success program. Social validity of the First Step to Success program and treatment integrity of the intervention were also examined.

Child Behavior Checklist (CBCL; Achenbach, 1978)

The Child Behavior Checklist has been an empirically based means of screening children for behavior disorders (Achenbach, 1991a; Achenbach & Edelbrock, 1978). It is developed to assess in a standardized format the behavioral problems and social competencies of children as reported by parents. Clinical scales have been refined through factor-analytic techniques. Cutting scores for the scales have also been given to establish significant behavioral psychopathology (Achenbach & Edelbrock, 1978, 1983). The Turkish version of CBCL has been shown to be a reliable and valid scale in Turkey as well as in the U.S.

The CBCL takes about 20 minutes for parents to complete and consists of 118 behavioral and 20 social competence items. Parents rate their child's behavior on a three-point scale; whether each behavioral item is not true (scored as 0), somewhat or sometimes true (scored as 1), or very true or often true (scored as 2) of their child's behavior over the past 6 months.

The Child Behavior Checklist also consists of two pages of questions concerning the child's social activities and social interaction. Information from these two pages yields scores for social competency scales. The Scoring profile has separate normative data for each sex, at ages 4 to 5, 6 to 11, and 12 to 16 years.

The Attention Problems scale assesses a hyperactivity and inattention dimension of child behavior. Studies show an association between the Attention Problems scale and the diagnosis of attention-deficit hyperactive disorder (AD/HD) Shekim et al. (1986) and Edelbrock and Costello (1988). In addition, Weinstein, Noam, Grimes, Stone, and Schwab-Stone (1990) showed that children with AD/HD had elevations on CBCL scales in addition to hyperactivity. These elevations were associated with comorbid disorders among the children with AD/HD.

Back translation, bilingual retest method, and pretest field study were done for CBCL

(Erol, Arslan, & Akcakin, 1995). The test-retest reliability of the Turkish form was 0.84 for Total

Problems. Internal consistency of the Turkish version form was adequate (Cronbach's

alpha+0.88) (Erol, Arslan, & Akcakin, 1995).

Teacher Report Form (TRF; Achenbach, 1991b)

The Teacher's Report Form (Edelbrock & Achenbach, 1984) is a scale intended for

teachers to complete to describe children's behavior relative to their same-age peers. The TRF is

modeled after the CBCL and it obtains teachers' reports of children's academic performance,

adaptive functioning, and behavioral/emotional problems. This 113-item questionnaire provided

for recording teacher observations of the child's academic progress and overall functioning

within the classroom, has become the standard in child research. The TRF can be used with

students ages 5 through 18.

Teachers should have interacted with the child on a daily basis for approximately two

months before completing this questionnaire. The TRF are divided into eight or nine behavioral

scales, depending on the child's age and sex. These scales deal with specific empirically derived

childhood categories. The TRF Test Manual adequately provides reliable and valid evidence for

its use as a measure of children's problem behaviors. Test–retest reliabilities ranging from 1 to 4

weeks between ratings were reported to be .90 to .92, and numerous concurrent and predictive

validity studies document its validity in identifying students experiencing emotional and

behavioral difficulties (Achenbach, 1991b).

Achenbach (1996) recently reported a strong relationship between TRF's empirically

derived scales and the categorical diagnostic system of DSM-IV. Scales on the TRF form include

withdrawn, somatic complaints, anxious/depressed, social problems, thought problems, attention

65

roblems, delinquent behavior, and aggressive behavior.

Back translation, bilingual retest method, and pretest field study were done for TRF Erol, Arslan, & Akcakin, 1995). The test-retest reliability of the Turkish form was 0.88 for Total roblems. Internal consistency of the Turkish version form was adequate (Cronbach's lpha+0.87) (Erol, Arslan, & Akcakin, 1995).

Several behavior-rating scales have been developed to assess attention leficit/hyperactivity disorder symptoms. Broadband rating scales are comprehensive and span he internalizing and externalizing symptomotologies. The CBCL and TRF of CBCL are two amples of broadband rating scales. If a broad band measurement indicates deviance in AD/HD-elated domains, narrow band instruments yields specific information about AD/HD yptomology to examine the disorder more directly. ADHD Rating Scale-IV is a well-respected cale and has been used in the field of AD/HD research commonly.

D/HD Rating Scale-IV (DuPaul, Power, Anastopoulos, and Reid, 1998)

The ADHD Rating Scale-IV was developed by George DuPaul, Thomas Power, Arthur Anastopoulos, and Robert Reid (1998). The questionere is a revision of the previously published ADHD Rating Scale-IV and its 18 items were adapted directly from the AD/HD symptom list as pecified in the DSM-IV. It was designed to obtain parent and teacher information regarding the requency of the symptoms related to attention deficit/hyperactivity disorder as indicated by the DSM-IV (DuPaul et al., 1998).

There is a home version of the ADHD Rating Scale-IV that parents complete and a chool version that teachers complete. The respondents are requested to select the single esponse for each item that best described the frequency of the specific behavior displayed by the arget child over the past 6 months or since the beginning of the school year. The frequency of

66

each item or symptom was delineated on a 4-point Likert scale ranging from never or rarely (0) to very often (3), with higher scores indicative of greater AD/HD-related behavior. In order to address possible response bias, Inattention symptoms were designated as odd-numbered items and Hyperactivity-Impulsivity symptoms were displayed as even-numbered items (DuPaul et al., 1998).

The ADHD Rating Scale-IV School and Home Versions are reported to have adequate psychometric properties for use as a screening, diagnostic, and treatment outcome measure (DuPaul et al., 1998; DuPaul, Power, McGoey, Ikeda, & Anastopoulos, 1997; Power et al., 1998). To measure internal consistency reliability, coefficient alphas were calculated. The results were as follows: Total score, 94; Inattention, .96; and Hyperactivity-Impulsivity, .88. Pearson product-moment correlation coefficients: Total Score, .90; Inattention, .89; and Hyperactivity-Impulsivity, .88 (DuPaul et al., 1998). The teacher ratings scale and the parent ratings scale and the combination of the parent and teacher ratings were found to have adequate positive and negative predictive power in the diagnosis of AD/HD (Power et al., 1998).

ADHD Rating Scale-IV translated into Turkish by the researcher and peer reviewed for the language accuracy. Since 18 items of ADHD Rating Scale-IV in English version were adapted directly from the AD/HD symptom list as specified in the DSM-IV, the Turkish version of DSM-IV was used in the translations.

Teacher Ratings of Behavior (Perkins-Rowe, 2001)

Teacher Ratings of Behavior is a survey that evaluates the effectiveness of the program on the class-wide student behaviors and teacher behaviors. It is designed to evaluate the effectiveness of the program on the class-wide student behaviors and teacher behaviors. The survey consists of two sub-scales based on class-wide student behaviors and teacher behaviors.

The subscale with respect to class-wide student behaviors is composed of 15 items while the subscale with respect to teacher behaviors is composed of 5 items. The participant teachers rate each item using a 5-point Likert-type scale ranging from 1 (none) to 3 (a few times) to 5 (very often).

Interviews

Adults who work directly with a target child have a wealth of stored knowledge about that student's "typical" behaviors and changes on her behaviors during the implementation of an intervention. Therefore, teacher and parent interviews are of great value in the evaluation of the effectiveness of the First Step to Success program and potential cultural barriers of the Program. In order to learn the cumulative knowledge base of adults closely associated with the child, semi-structured interviews with teachers and parents were conducted in this study.

The interviews were planned to be conducted using a semi-structured format; that is, questions included in this interview do not have to be asked verbatim but may be stated in the consultant's own words. The main advantage of the semi-structured interview is that it allows the interviewer to bring a standardized set of questions to each interview while sustaining the flexibility to react with specific follow up questions to unique information provided by the parents or teachers.

Semi-structured teacher and parent interviews were performed in order to gain more detailed information about the effectiveness of the First Step to Success program and feasibility and cultural barriers of the First Step to Success program.

Experimental Design and Procedures

A single-subject, multiple-baseline design across subjects (Cooper, Heron, & Heward, 1987; Kazdin, 1982; Tawney & Gast, 1984) was utilized for this study. Multiple baseline designs display the effect of a treatment by showing that more than one baseline changes as a consequence of a treatment. By examining more than one baseline, effects of confounds from other variables are reduced. Thus, a multiple baselines across groups design introduces the treatment at a different time for each group of participants (Tawney & Gast, 1984).

A multiple-baseline, across-groups design was selected for the following reasons.

1. The design does not require a return to baseline condition in order to show experimental control.

2. The multiple-baseline design permits the measurement of an independent variable across groups of subjects.

3. The design allows the researcher the opportunity to understand the relationship of the independent variable on behaviors across groups of students.

Screening Phase

In order to have a subject pool comprised of children who had been clinically diagnosed with AD/HD, a permission letter from the Turkish Ministry of National Education for the study was provided to Guidance and Research Center in Sincan school district in Ankara, the capital city of Turkey. Sincan school district was selected for this study due to low socio-economic level of its population. The literature has reported a high frequency of AD/HD among children from families of a low socio-economic level. In fact, it has been documented that, AD/HD in children are most likely to be due to a complex interaction between biological risk factors and environmental risk factors (Johnston & Mash, 2001).

The guidance and research centers in Turkey typically have records of most students with AD/HD in their district. Because legally in Turkey, when a teacher has concerns about a particular student who might have AD/HD, she or he notifies the parents to take the child to the district guidance and research center for the initial assessment. These centers are responsible for keeping the records of children who had been referred to the centers. The basic information about a referred child such as the name of the child and school is accessible for researchers who have necessary permission from Ministry of National Education.

After gathering a pool of students with AD/HD, the teachers of the students with AD/HD were contacted and informed about the study. The Student Risk Screening Scale-SRSS developed by Drummond (as cited in Walker, Stiller, Golly, Kavanagh, Severson, & Feil, 1997), was given to the teachers to rate students showing obvious signs of antisocial behavior patterns in their classrooms. Initially teachers were not informed that they were contacted since they had a student with AD/HD in their classroom. The teachers screened all the students in their classrooms on a set of behavioral criteria that are strongly associated with antisocial behavior patterns. Children with AD/HD who were rated 15 or higher scores in the class were considered candidates for the First Step to Success program. Candidate children and their parents were contacted to give detailed information about the study. Children who provided both parent consent and child assent were eligible to join the study.

Baseline Phase

In this study, participant children were divided into two groups. Group 1 (G1) were composed of two participant first grade students whereas Group 2 (G2) were composed of two first grade students. Observations of participant children's academic agreement behaviors were recorded daily for 30 minutes in the classroom. A time-sampling technique (Kerr & Nelson, 1989) was used to record behaviors of the students during instructional periods. The time-sampling procedure involves dividing the class period into one minute intervals and then recording the observational data at the end of each interval. Gathering of baseline data began at the same time for both groups and were made simultaneously across participant groups till baseline data across all participant student groups displayed acceptable stability in level and trend on academic engagement behaviors. Following the gathering of baseline data, the intervention was implemented to Group 1 while Group 2 stayed in baseline. On the implementation day 6, the intervention for G2 began.

Intervention Phase

A First Step to Success program consultant sets up the program, initially implements, and coordinates from start to finish over a 3-month period. Following the baseline phase the program consultant begins implementation of CLASS and HomeBase components of the program. The school intervention component of the First Step to Success program, CLASS, takes 30 program days and begins with a five-day consultant phase. On Day 6, the teacher phase begins. Now the classroom teacher carries out the program with support and supervision provided by the consultant. The teacher phase of the program lasts until Day 20. In teacher phase, the target child learns to work toward less frequent but higher magnitude backup rewards at school and home. The teacher also communicates with parents on a regular basis with regard to the target child's performance. The Maintenance Phase of the CLASS program lasts from program day 21 to 30. In this final program phase, the target child's improved behavior is rewarded primarily with praise and expressions of approval from the teacher and the parents. The HomeBase component of the First Step to Success begins on program Day 10 of the CLASS and continues once a week for six weeks. Daily observations of participant children's academic engagement behaviors will continue for 30 minutes in order to gather data.

Post-Intervention/Follow-up Phase

Post-intervention data was comprised of follow up data. Follow up data was obtained on

71

target children's academic engagement behaviors with three 30 minutes daily observations at three months. Teacher and parents ratings on the target children's social emotional problems and teacher and parent ratings on the target children's problem behaviors were included in the follow up data in order to evaluate the effects of the First Step to Success program on target children.

Intervention Procedures

As an initial step, the principal researcher got training in the specifics of the program at the Institute on Violence and Destructive Behavior at the University of Oregon. The principal researcher then translated the First Step to Success program into Turkish and obtained a written approval which showed that the translated version was linguistically and conceptually equivalent to the original version from Turkish Ministry of National Education. Following the translation, the researcher was responsible for implementing and coordinating the First Step to Success program in Turkey.

Prior to the implementation of the First Step to Success program, necessary training was provided to the participant teachers by the principal researcher. The training was addressed the key components of the First Step to Success program, implementation procedure, responsibilities of the participant teachers and principal researcher, and the use of RED/GREEN card during the implementation. Teacher's questions and concerns related to the program were also discussed to ensure that the participant teachers were able to master their responsibilities and implement the program effectively under the principal researcher's supervision. In addition, the teachers set up the first meeting with participant children's parents in order to solicit parental support and involvement in the program. Participant parents were explained about specifics of the First Step to Success program including HomeBase as well as CLASS. The principal researcher assisted parents to understand their roles and responsibilities in the program and how to effectively

72

establish school home partnership. Additionally, the teachers and consultant talked to parents about their observations about their child's behavior and discussed (1) the child's appropriate behaviors, (2) behaviors that need improvement, (3) behaviors that were problems. Following that, behaviors that need to be learned and problem behaviors that need to be eliminated were discussed. Finally target behaviors and goals were identified by the consultant, teachers and parents.

In the next step, the consultant met with the each child individually and explained the program. The primary purposes of this meeting were to explain the program to the child and obtain the child's agreement to participate. The consultant then clarified the expected behaviors and rewards for these behaviors. After the initial meetings with the teacher, parents and child, the consultant set up the CLASS program for G1, runed it, and showed its implementation and effectiveness to the classroom teacher for the first five program days. On Day 6, the consultant turned implementation over the teacher with support and supervision provided by the consultant. The HomeBase component took place on Program Day 11 for G1. On the Program Day 6 for G1, gathering baseline data for G2 was finished and the CLASS was started. The HomeBase component with G2 was started on the Program Day 11 with G2.

During implementation of the First Step to Success program, the consultant was responsible for coordination and ensuring the effective implementation of the Class and the HomeBase components. In addition, the consultant provided teachers and parents with necessary support in a consultative capacity and showed the effectiveness of the CLASS for teachers in the most intensive part of the program. Following the most intensive part of the program, the consultant met with the teachers daily and reviewed the targeted children's performance on that day and generally in the program. The consultant also helped solve problems as needed and

73

acilitated communication between the teachers and the parents.

Observation and Coding Procedures

For the purpose of this study, student academic engagement behaviors were observed rough children's on task and off task active and passive behaviors. The principal researcher and one trained graduate student recorded data on student behavior during 30 minutes lessons in each program day. The teacher conducted the lesson, and interacted with the target student in her usual manner. A time-sampling technique (Kerr & Nelson, 1989) was used to record behavior of the children during instructional periods. The Time-sampling procedure involved dividing the class period into one minute intervals and then recording the observational data at the end of each interval. Behaviors of each student were recorded at the end of the first minute and the end of each minute thereafter for up to thirty minutes.

The observation system involved three categories of behavior: on-task; off-task, active; and off-task, passive. Descriptions of the behaviors included under each code will be provided as follow. (1) On-Task. On-Task was characterized by general orientation toward the teacher, working on assigned paper-pencil tasks, task-relevant talking, reading class materials, and listening to the teacher or other students' task relevant talking. (2) Off-Task, Active. Off-task, active, was characterized by drumming pencils, hands or feet, playing with toys, or being out of area without permission. Incidental motor behaviors which do not distract other students or prevent other students from attending to instruction, such as idly swinging the foot on a crossed leg or quietly stretching are not included as off-task behaviors under this category. Verbal off-task behaviors characterized by talking, singing, humming, and verbal noises not related to task were also included in this category. (3) Off-task passive. Off-task, passive behaviors included students laying their heads on the desk, looking out windows, staring at the ceiling, sleeping, and

74

passive refusal to participate in the class such as ignoring the teacher.

Observations were conducted during baseline, intervention, and post intervention/follow up phases of the study. During the baseline phase, observations were taken and recorded until a pattern of stable performance was established for G1 (student 1 and student 2). Due to the multiple baseline design, baseline data for G2 (student 3 and student 4) was taken after baseline was collected for G1. Observation data was carried out during each program day for G1 and G2. During the follow up phase, three daily observations were also collected for each participant children.

Interrater Reliability

In order to have interrater reliability, the principal researcher and a trained graduate student collected the observational data for each participant student. The trained graduate student coded 30% of the observational data for 9 days for reliability. A time-sampling technique (Kerr & Nelson, 1989) was used to record behavior of the students during instructional periods. The Time-sampling procedure involved dividing the class period into one minute intervals and then recording the observational data at the end of each interval. Behaviors of each student were recorded at the end of the first minute and the end of each minute thereafter for up to thirty minutes.

The principal researcher and one trained graduate student recorded data on student behavior during 30 minutes lessons in each program day. The teacher conducted the lesson, and interacted with the target student in her usual manner. Agreements were calculated by dividing the number of intervals in which the observers agreed by the number of agreements plus disagreements and multiplying by 100.

75

An interrater reliability coefficient of .80 was required between coders. Percentage scores for reliability of academic engagement time for Student 1 ranged from 80 to 100 with a mean of 90.7; for Student 2 ranged from 83 to 99 with a mean of 91.2; for Student 3 ranged from 80 to 99 with a mean of 89.4; and for Student 4 ranged from 88 to 97 with a mean of 89.2.

Collection of Other Data

The dependent measures used in this study included CBCL, TRF, and ADHD Rating Scale-IV Rating Scale-IV. In order to see the intervention outcomes, CBCL, TRF, and ADHD Rating Scale-IV were collected on participant children's social emotional problems and problem behaviors as pre-intervention data. Same measures were used to assess the effects of the First Step to Success program immediately after program completion. These measures were also administered to the participant teachers and parents three months after the program completion as follow up data. Furthermore, semi-structured interviews with parents and teachers were conducted with participant teachers and parents to explore their perspectives on the effectiveness of the First Step to Success program and feasibility of the First Step to Success program in Turkish culture. Finally, a survey was taken with participant teachers and parents in order to evaluate their satisfaction of the program and social validity of the program.

Treatment Integrity

A two-hour teacher training was provided to the participant teachers prior to the implementation of the First Step to Success program. The training offered necessary knowledge on the key components of the First Step to Success program, implementation procedure, responsibilities of the participant teachers and principal researcher, and the use of RED/GREEN card during the implementation. Teachers' questions and concerns related to the program were also discussed to ensure that the participant teachers were able to master their responsibilities and

76

implement the program effectively under the principal researcher's supervision.

In addition, there was a significant need for high-quality implementation in achieving successful outcomes. If the program consultant, teachers and parents were not committed to the program fidelity, they might be utilizing a great deal of valuable time and resources with little to no effect on the behaviors they were trying to change. Therefore the fidelity implementation analyses were conducted by the Monitoring Form provided by the program in order to obtain a measure of treatment integrity and the returned GREEN/RED cards from home. The monitoring form was used by the consultant and teacher to record the target student's daily progress through the First Step CLASS component. In every treatment phase of the program, the consultant was responsible to review the treatment components to ensure that all the intended components of the intervention were actually implemented as planned. Lack of or weak intervention effects might be the result of failing to implement interventions as intended. The number of program days in which components of the intervention were actually implemented as planned were divided by total of program days, and then multiplied by 100 to obtain the percentage of treatment integrity for each teacher. The percentage of treatment integrity was 94.7 for Teacher 1; 93.4 for Teacher 2; 80.3 for Teacher 3; and 100 for Teacher 4.

Social Validity

To evaluate the social validity of the First Step to Success program, a satisfaction survey developed by Perkins-Rowe (as cited in Diken, 2004) for the First Step to Success program was collected to assess parent and teacher levels of satisfaction with the program. Specific questions reflecting attitudes toward program was addressed using a 5-point scale. Teacher Satisfaction Survey involved 13 items related to teachers' satisfaction and perceptions with regard to the ease of implementation of the First Step to Success program. Parent's Satisfaction Survey was

77

dapted from the Teacher Satisfaction Survey and consisted of 12 items. It was developed to valuate parents' satisfaction with the program.

In addition, results of the Teacher and Parent's Satisfaction surveys and semi-structured nterviews were reported qualitatively by discussing features of item responses.

Data Analysis

The primary analyses for the study question 1 and 2 involved the pretest, posttest, and ollow up data on CBCL, TRF, ADHD Rating Scale-IV, and observational data on participant hildren's academic engagement behaviors. For the observational data, the mean and range ercentage scores of academic engagement behaviors of participant children collected from daily bservations were calculated. Treatment effectiveness involving the study question 1 and 2 were larified through statistical and descriptive analysis of data with the use of SPSS and the results vere presented graphically.

Study questions 3 and 4 will also be analyzed through statistical and descriptive analysis f data collected from teachers by using the Teacher Ratings of Behavior. Finally, in order to nswer study question 5 and 6, qualitative analysis of the semi-structured interviews were erformed for a deeper understanding of teacher and parent perceptions on the effectiveness of he First Step to Success program.

CHAPTER IV

Results

Effectiveness of the FSS Program on Participant Children's Social Emotional Problems

A multiple baseline across groups research design was used to evaluate the effectiveness of the FSS program. Data from four different measures were collected in order to examine the impact of the FSS program on participant children's social emotional and problem behaviors: ADHD Rating Scale-IV (at baseline, before and after the intervention), CBCL (at baseline, before and after the intervention), TRF (at baseline, before and after the intervention), and Observational data (daily observations at baseline, during and after the intervention).

Initially in this study, the Turkish version of the Social Skills Rating System (SSRS) was planned to use to evaluate the effectiveness of the First Step to Success program on target children's social skills problems. However, the Turkish version of the SSRS was not accessible at the time of the study due to the long waiting time to get a permission to use the instrument.

The following section will summarize the individual findings of the participant children's individual findings on the Childhood Behavior Checklist (CBCL) and Teacher Report Form (TRF).

Childhood Behavior Checklist (CBCL) Results

The Child Behavior Checklist (CBCL; Achenbach, 1991) was used to assess emotional and behavioral problems in participant children. This behavioral rating scale includes items about activities, social relationships, academic performance, chores, and hobbies, which are summarized in three competence scales: Activities, Social and School scales. CBCL also has eight empirically-validated syndromes including Withdrawn, Somatic Complaints, Anxious/ Depressed, Social Problems, Thought Problems, Attention Problems, Delinquent Behavior, and Aggressive. For more information on CBCL please refer to the Chapter III, the methods on page 72.

Mert.

The results of the parent ratings on CBCL showed that Mert was in the clinical range both in the Competence scale (6.5, T= 18) and the Problem Behavior scales (T=74). On the Problem Behavior scales, Mert showed the greatest deviance on the Attention scale with an exceptionally high T score (19, T= 96), followed by the Aggressive Problems scale (T=81), Rule-Breaking Behavior Scale (T= 70), and the Social Problem scale (T= 69) which was on the borderline clinical range.

After the completion of the program, Parents' post intervention ratings on the CBCL revealed increase on the competence scales and significant decrease on the problem scales. On the Competence scales, Mert's CBCL score for activities remained in the clinical range (T=12.5). However his social score of 5 and his school score of 3.5 increased to the normal range.

Mert displayed a dramatic decrease on his problem behavior scales (34, T=57) which was well in the normal range. More specifically, Mert's Attention Problems scale score dropped to 10 (T=66) borderline clinical range, his Aggressive Problems scale score dropped to 11 (T= 64) normal range, his Rule Breaking Behavior scale score dropped to 1 (T=51) normal range, and his Social Problems scale score dropped to 2 (T=54) which was well within the normal range.

Behavioral improvements maintained during the follow up phase as well. Mert's Competence scales score increased slightly but remained in the clinical range (14, T=27). On the other hand, his Problem scale scores continued to decrease remaining in the normal range (32, T= 56).

Oguz.

Parent ratings of the CBCL on the baseline showed that Oguz was in the clinical range on both Competence scale (14, T= 27) and Problem Behaviors scale (70, T=71). On the Problem Behavior scales, Oguz showed the greatest deviance on the Attention (T= 83), followed by Aggressive Problems scale (T=78), and Social Problems scale (T= 67).

As soon as the intervention initiated, an immediate positive decrease on Oguz's problem behaviors were observed. His competence scale score increased to 23 (T=47) well within the normal range. His Total problem scales score drooped to 31 (T=55), normal range. More specifically, Oguz's Attention Problems scale score drooped to 10 (T=66) borderline clinical range, his Aggressive Problems scale score drooped to 10 (T= 62) normal range, and his Social Problems scale score dropped to 3 (T=56) well within the normal range.

During the follow up phase, Oguz's Competence scales score continued to be high (T=48) well within the normal range. His Problem scale scores increased slightly, but remained in the normal range (T= 59).

Selim.

The results of the parent ratings on CBCL showed that, Selim was in the clinical range in both Competence scales (T= 27) and Problem Behavior scales (T=74). On the Problem Behavior scales, Selim showed the greatest deviance on the Attention scale with an exceptionally high T score (T= 96), followed by Aggressive Problems scale (T=75), and Social Problem scale (T= 69) which was in the borderline clinical range.

On the postintervention phase, parent ratings on the CBCL revealed significant increase on the Competence Scales and significant decrease on the Problem Behavior scales. Selim's competence scale score increased to 21 (T=41), well within the normal range. His Total Problem scales score drooped to 37 (T=59), which was in the normal range. More specifically, Selim' Attention Problems scale score drooped to 12 (T=69) borderline clinical range, his Aggressive Problems scale score drooped to 11 (T= 64), normal range, and his Social Problems scale score dropped to 4 (T=64) which was on the normal range.

Furthermore, behavioral improvements maintained during the follow up phase. Selim's Competence scales score continued to be high (21, T=41) well within the normal range. His Problem scale scores increased slightly, but remained in the normal range (36, T= 58).

Serhat.

Parent ratings of the CBCL on the Baseline showed that Serhat was in clinical range on both Competence scale (7.5, T= 19) and Problem Behaviors scale (72, T=72). On the Problem Behavior scales, Serhat showed the greatest deviance on the Attention scale with an exceptionally high T score (T= 85), followed by Aggressive Problems scale (T=75), and Social Problems scale (T= 70).

Postintervention parent ratings on the CBCL indicated that Serhat showed significant increase on the Competence scale and significant decrease on the Problem Behavior scale. Serhat's Competence scale score increased to 22 (T=44) well within the normal range. His Total Problem scales score dropped to 32 (T=56), which was in the normal range. More specifically,

Serhat's Attention Problems scale score dropped to 9 (T=64) normal range, his Aggressive Problems scale score dropped to 9 (T= 61) normal range, his Rule-Breaking Behavior problems dropped to 1 (T=51) normal range and his Social Problems scale score dropped to 4 (T=58) normal range.

Furthermore, behavioral improvements maintained during the follow up phase. Serhat's Competence scales score continued to be high (22, T=44) well within the normal range. His Problem scale scores also remained in the normal range (34, T= 57).

Table 3

Parents' ratings on the subscales of the CBCL

CBCL Scales Raw Scores

	Withdrawn			Somatic Comp.			Anxious/Depres.			Social Problems			Thought Prob.			Attention Prob.			Delinquent Beh.			Aggressive Beh.			Total		
	Pre	Post	F	Pre	Post	F	Pre	Post	F	Pre	Post	F	Pre	Post	F	Pre	Post	F	Pre	Post	F	Pre	Post	F	Pre	Post	F
Parent 1	7	2	0	0	0	0	4	1	1	9	2	2	4	2	3	19	10	9	7	1	1	24	11	12	74	34	32
Parent 2	4	2	3	0	0	0	5	1	2	8	3	4	3	2	3	16	10	11	5	0	0	22	10	12	70	31	37
Parent 3	4	2	2	2	0	0	6	2	0	9	4	5	6	2	3	19	12	13	5	0	1	20	11	11	82	37	36
Parent 4	2	1	1	0	0	0	4	2	1	7	4	2	4	2	2	17	9	11	9	1	1	31	9	10	64	32	30

84

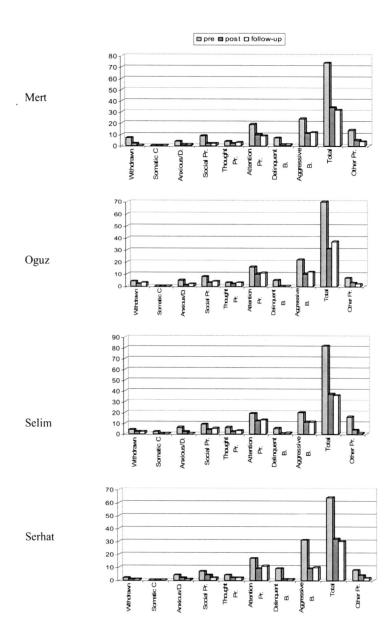

Figure 1. Parents' Pre, Post, and Follow-up student ratings on the CBCL.

Teacher Report Form (TRF) Results

The Teacher Report Form (TRF) is designed to obtain teachers' reports of children's academic performance, adaptive functioning, and behavioral/emotional problems. The TRF has 118 problem items, of which 93 have counterparts on the CBCL/6-18. The remaining items concern school behaviors that parents would not observe, such as difficulty following directions, disturbs other pupils, and disrupts class discipline. Teachers rate the child for how true each item is now or was within the past two months, using the same three-point response scale as for the CBCL/6-18. For more information on TRF please refer to the Chapter III, the methods on page 73.

Mert.

The profile scored from the TRF completed by Mert's classroom teacher on the baseline showed statistical deviance both on the Total Problem scale (T=82) and Adaptive Functioning scale (T=35). On the Problem Behavior scales Mert's teacher reflected the greatest deviance on the Aggressive Behavior scale with an exceptionally high T score (T=96), followed by the Attention Problems (T= 88), Social Problems (T=79), and Delinquent Behaviors (T=78) scales.

As soon as the intervention initiated, an immediate positive decrease on Mert's problem behaviors were observed. His Adaptive Functioning scale score increased to 13 (T=41) which was in the normal range. His Total Problem scales score dropped to 37 (T=58), which was also well within the normal range. More specifically, Mert's Aggressive Behavior scale score dropped to10 (T= 62) normal range, his Attention Problems scale score dropped to 12 (T=55) normal range, his Social Problems scale score dropped to 4 (T=61) normal range, and his Delinquent Behaviors scale score dropped to 3 (T=60) well within the normal range.

During the follow up phase, Mert's Adaptive Functioning scale score continued to be high 13 (T=41) well within the normal range and his Problem scale score continued to be in the normal range 38 (T= 58).

Oguz.

The results of the teacher ratings on TRF showed that, Oguz was in the clinical range both on the Adaptive Functioning scale 11(T= 37) and Total Problem Behavior scales 109 (T=78). On the Problem Behavior scales, Oguz showed the greatest deviance on the Aggressive Behavior scale 43 (T=90), followed by the Social Problem scale 17 (T= 83), and the Attention Problems scale 30 (T=73).

On the postintervention phase, teacher ratings on the TRF revealed significant increase on the Adaptive Functioning scale and significant decrease on the Total Problem scales. His Adaptive Functioning scale score increased to 13 (T=41) well within the normal range. His Total Problem scales score dropped to 33 (T=56) normal range. More specifically, Oguz's Aggressive Behavior scale score dropped to 9 (T= 68), his Social Problems scale score dropped to 7 (T=66) which was in the normal range and his Attention Problems scale score dropped to 10 (T=52) well within the normal range.

Behavioral improvements maintained during the follow up phase. Oguz's Adaptive Functioning scale score continued to be high (19, T=53) well within the normal range. His Total Problem scales scores also remained in the normal range (35, T= 58).

Selim.

Teacher ratings of the TRF on the Baseline showed that Selim was in clinical range on both Adaptive Functioning scale (9, T= 35) and Total Problem scales (144, T=87). On the Problem scales, Selim showed the greatest deviance on the Attention Problems scale (T=94), ollowed by Social Problems scale (T= 88), and Aggressive Behavior scale (T=83).

Postintervention teacher ratings on the TRF indicated that Selim showed significant ncrease on the Adaptive Functioning scale and slight decrease on the Problem Scales. Selim's Adaptive Functioning scale score increased to 14 (T=41) within the normal range. His Total Problem scales score dropped to 70 (T=67), which was still in the clinical range. More pecifically, Selim's Attention Problems scale score dropped to 23 (T=63) normal range, his Aggressive Problems scale score dropped to 26 (T= 67) borderline clinical range, and his Social Problems scale score dropped to 10 (T=70) which was in the borderline clinical range. It should e noted that, according to his teacher, Selim continued to display some aggressive behaviors particularly on the playground, a setting where other children attempted to tease him frequently, behavioral expectations were not clear as in the classroom, and were not always observable.

During the follow up phase, Selim's Adaptive Functioning scales score continued to be igh (13, T=41) normal range. His problem scales showed a slight decrease, though still emaining in the clinical range (67, T= 65).

Serhat.

On the baseline, the profile scored from the TRF completed by Serhat's classroom eacher showed deviance both on the Total Problem scale (131, T=84) and Adaptive Functioning cales (6, T=35). On the Problem Behavior scales Serhat's teacher reported the greatest deviance n the Attention Problems (37, T= 91) and on the Delinquent Behavior (15, T=91) scales, ollowed by Aggressive Problems (43, T=90), and Social Problems scales (16, T=79).

As soon as the intervention initiated, an immediate positive decrease on Serhat's problem behaviors were observed. His Adaptive Functioning scale score increased to 15 (T=45) which vas in the normal range. His Total Problem scales score dropped to 42 (T=58) normal range.

88

More specifically, Serhat's Attention Problems scale score dropped to 13 (T=56) normal range, his Delinquent Behavior scale score dropped to 5 (T=66) normal range, his Aggressive Problems scale score dropped to13 (T= 59) normal range, and his Social Problems scale score dropped to 4 (T=61) normal range.

During the follow up phase, Serhat's Adaptive Functioning scale score continued to be high 16 (T=47), well within the normal range and his Problem scale score remained in the normal range (40, T= 58).

Table 4

Teachers' ratings on the subscales of the TRF

	TRF Scale raw scores																										
	Withdrawn			Somatic Comp.			Anxious/Depres.			Social Problems			Thought Prob.			Attention Prob.			Delinquent Beh.			Aggressive Beh.			Total		
	Pre	Post	F	Pre	Post	F	Pre	Post	F	Pre	Post	F	Pre	Post	F	Pre	Post	F	Pre	Post	F	Pre	Post	F	Pre	Post	F
Teacher 1	0	0	0	0	0	0	9	3	2	15	4	3	1	1	0	36	12	13	10	3	4	47	10	13	126	37	38
Teacher 2	0	0	0	0	0	0	8	4	1	17	7	4	1	0	0	30	10	10	5	2	2	43	9	16	109	33	33
Teacher 3	5	2	1	2	1	2	13	3	4	20	10	8	4	1	0	39	23	22	5	2	2	38	26	24	144	70	67
Teacher 4	2	1	0	0	0	0	7	2	2	15	4	4	2	1	0	37	13	12	15	5	4	43	13	14	131	42	40

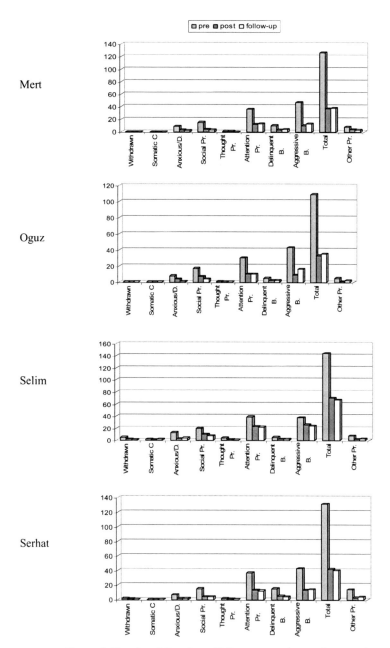

Figure 2. Teachers' Pre, Post, Follow-up student ratings on the TRF.

ADHD Rating Scale-IV Results

ADHD Rating Scale-IV was used to obtain teacher information regarding the frequency of the symptoms related to attention deficit/hyperactivity disorder as indicated by the DSM-IV. The questionere has 18 items that were adapted directly from the AD/HD symptom list as specified in the DSM-IV. For more information on ADHD Rating Scale-IV please refer to the chapter III, the methods on page 75.

Mert.

Mert was a 7 year old first-grade boy who was diagnosed with AD/HD Combined subtype. Teacher ratings on the ADHD Rating Scale-IV indicated that he was at the 89th percentile with a raw score of 20 on the Inattention subscale, at the 98th percentile with a raw score of 27 on the Hyperactivity-Impulsivity subscale, and at the 98th percentile with a raw score of 47 on the Total Scores. Teacher ratings on both Inattention and Hyperactivity-Impulsivity subscales strongly suggested the presence of ADHD.

As soon as the intervention began, the problem behavior associated with AD/HD was significantly reduced and positive behaviors such as following directions without being disruptive or aggressive, staying seated, working on-tasks, and participating in class activities were significantly increased. After the intervention ended, the post-intervention data were gathered from the classroom teacher to determine the effectiveness of FSS program on Mert. Teacher ratings revealed that Mert was at the 50th percentile with a raw score of 11 on the Inattention subscale, at the 50th percentile with a raw score of 12 on the Hyperactivity-Impulsivity subscale, and at the 50th percentile with a raw score of 23 on the Total Scores. Comparisons of these scores with those observed during the initial assessment yielded RCIs of

2.51 (Inattention), 3.64 (Hyperactivity-Impulsivity), and 3.68 (Total). These results showed that observed improvements in Mert's Inattention and Hyperactivity-Impulsivity symptoms were due to the FSS program.

Reliable Change Index (RCI) is a procedure for assessing clinical significance and it was developed by Jacobson and Truax (1991). RCI is equal to the difference between a child's pretreatment score and postreatment score, divided by the standard error of difference between the two test scores. When the RCI exceeds 1.96, it is unlikely that the change from pretreatment to posttreatment is due change. Therefore, the RCI functions as a measure of the degree to which an improvement in behaviors is likely due to the effects of treatment rather than to imprecise measurement.

Furthermore, during the follow-up assessment Mert's Inattention score was 11 with a 50%, his Hyperactivity-Impulsivity score was 13 with a 50%, and his Total score was 24 with a 50%. Comparisons of these scores with those observed during the initial assessment yielded RCIs of 2.51, 3.64, and 3.52. These results once again suggested strong evidence of statistically reliable change in terms of Mert's Inattention and Hyperactive-Impulsive symptoms were due to FSS early intervention program.

Table 5

Raw scores and RCI scores of Mert on the subscales of ADHD Rating Scale-IV

| | Mert | | | | |
| | Baseline | Intervention | | Follow-up | |
	Raw Scores	Raw Scores	RCI	Raw Scores	RCI
Inattention	20	11	2.51	11	2.51
Hyperactivity/Impulsivity	27	12	3.64	13	3.64
Total Scores	47	23	3.68	24	3.52

Oguz.

Oguz was a 7 year old first-grade boy who was diagnosed with AD/HD Combined subtype. Preintervention teacher ratings on the ADHD Rating Scale-IV were at the 75th percentile on the Inattention subscale with a raw score of 15, at the 94th percentile on the Hyperactivity-Impulsivity subscale with a raw score of 23, and at the 93rd percentile on the Total Scores with a raw score of 38. Teacher ratings on the Hyperactivity-Impulsivity subscale strongly suggested the presence of ADHD.

Post-intervention ratings were at the 50th percentile with a raw score of 8 on the Inattention subscale, at the 50th percentile on the Hyperactivity-Impulsivity subscale with a raw score of 14, and at the 50th percentile on the Total Scores with a raw score of 22. The RCI calculations for the postintervention results yielded 1.95 on the Inattention subscale, 2.86 on the Hyperactivity-Impulsivity subscale, and 2.45 on the Total scores. Although there was a little evidence of statistically reliable change in terms of Oguz's Inattention symptoms, there was much reason to believe that the observed improvements in his Hyperactivity-Impulsivity symptoms were due to the FSS program.

In addition, follow-up teacher ratings on the ADHD Rating Scale-IV were at the 50 percentile with a raw score of 7 on the Inattention subscale, at the 50 percentile with a raw score of 13 on the Hyperactivity-Impulsivity subscale, and at the 50 percentile with a raw score of 20 on the Total scores. With closer inspection using RCI calculations for preintervetion-follow up assessment Oguz's Inattention, Hyperactivity-Impulsivity, and Total scores yielded RCIs of 1.95, 2.6, and 2.77. Thus, there continued to be a little evidence of statistically reliable change in terms of his Inattention symptoms, there was much reason to believe that the observed improvements in his Hyperactivity-Impulsivity symptoms were due to the FSS program.

Table 6

Raw scores and RCI scores of Oguz on the subscales of ADHD Rating Scale-IV

	Oguz					
	Baseline		Intervention		Follow-up	
	Raw Scores	RCI	Raw Scores	RCI	Raw Scores	RCI
Inattention	15		8	1.95	7	1.95
Hyperactivity/Impulsivity	23		14	2.86	13	2.6
Total Scores	38		22	2.45	20	2.77

Selim.

Selim was a 7-year old first grade boy who was diagnosed with AD/HD Combined subtype. Teacher ratings on the ADHD Rating Scale-IV indicated that he was at the 84th percentile, with a raw score of 21 on the Inattention subscale, at the 98th percentile with a raw score of 27 on the Hyperactivity-Impulsivity subscale, and at the 96th percentile with a raw score of 48 on the Total Scores. Teacher ratings on both Inattention and Hyperactivity-Impulsivity subscales strongly suggested the presence of AD/HD.

After the intervention ended, the postintervention data were gathered from the classroom teacher to determine the effectiveness of FSS program on the Selim. Teacher ratings revealed that Selim was at the 93th percentile with a raw score of 15 on the Inattention subscale, at the 97th percentile with a raw score of 21 on the Hyperactivity-Impulsivity subscale, and at the 96th percentile with a raw score of 36 on the Total Scores. Comparisons of these scores with those observed during the initial assessment yielded RCIs of 1.07 (Inattention), 1.57 (Hyperactivity-Impulsivity), and 1.88 (Total). Although Selim showed some improvements of his AD/HD symptoms, the improvements were not statistically significant. In other words the improvements were not sufficient to conclude that the FSS program was successful in decreasing Selim's AD/HD symptoms.

Furthermore, follow-up teacher ratings on the ADHD Rating Scale-IV were at the 93th percentile with a raw score of 15 on the Inattention subscale, at the 98th percentile with a raw score of 22 on the Hyperactivity-Impulsivity subscale, and at the 97th percentile with a raw score of 37 on the Total scores. The RCI calculations for the follow up data revealed scores of 1.07 (Inattention), 1.30 (Hyperactivity), and 1.68 (Total). These results showed that the decreases on Selim's AD/HD symptoms were not statistically significant. On the basis of these results, it was concluded that the improvements were not sufficient to conclude that the FSS program was successful in decreasing Selim's AD/HD symptoms.

Table 7

Raw scores and RCI scores of Selim on the subscales of ADHD Rating Scale-IV

	Selim					
	Baseline		Intervention		Follow-up	
	Raw Scores	RCI	Raw Scores	RCI	Raw Scores	RCI
Inattention	21		15	1.07	15	1.07
Hyperactivity/Impulsivity	27		21	1.57	22	1.3
Total Scores	48		36	1.88	37	1.68

Serhat.

Serhat was a first grade 7-year-old boy who was diagnosed with AD/HD Combined subtype. During Baseline, Serhat's teacher completed the ADHD Rating Scale-IV. His Inattention score was 20 with an 89% and his Hyperactivity-Impulsivity score was 23 with a 94%, and his Total score was 43 with a 93%. These scores indicated that Serhat was in the clinical range on ADHD Rating Scale-IV.

As soon as the intervention started, Serhat's positive behaviors such as following directions without being disruptive or aggressive, staying seated, working on-tasks, and participating in class activities were significantly increased and his problem behaviors associated to AD/HD were significantly reduced.

After the intervention ended, the postintervention data were gathered from the classroom teacher to determine the effectiveness of FSS program on Serhat. Teacher ratings revealed that

Serhat was at the 50th percentile with a raw score of 12 on the Inattention subscale, at the 50th percentile with a raw score of 12 on the Hyperactivity-Impulsivity subscale, and at the 50th percentile with a raw score of 24 on the Total Scores. At face value, these changes indicated the FSS intervention was effective in reducing his primary AD/HD symptomatology. With closer inspection using RCI calculations for preintervetion-postintervention, Serhat's Inattention, Hyperactivity-Impulsivity and Total scores yielded RCIs of 2.23, 2.86, and 2.91. These results showed that observed improvements in Serhat's Inattention and Hyperactivity-Impulsivity symptoms were due to the FSS program.

Three months after the intervention ended, Serhat's teacher once again rated his behavior. According to her follow-up ratings, Serhat's Inattention score was 12 with a 50%, his Hyperactivity-Impulsivity score was 10 with a 50%, and his Total score was 22 with a 50%. Comparisons of these scores with those observed during the initial assessment resulted RCIs of 2.23, 3.38, and 3.2. These results recommended a strong evidence of statistically reliable change in terms of Serhat's Inattention and Hyperactive-Impulsive symptoms were due to FSS early intervention program.

Table 8

Raw scores and RCI scores of Serhat on the subscales of ADHD Rating Scale-IV

	Serhat					
	Baseline		Intervention		Follow-up	
	Raw Scores	RCI	Raw Scores	RCI	Raw Scores	RCI
Inattention	20		12	2.23	12	2.23
Hyperactivity/Impulsivity	23		12	2.86	10	3.38
Total Scores	43		24	2.91	22	3.22

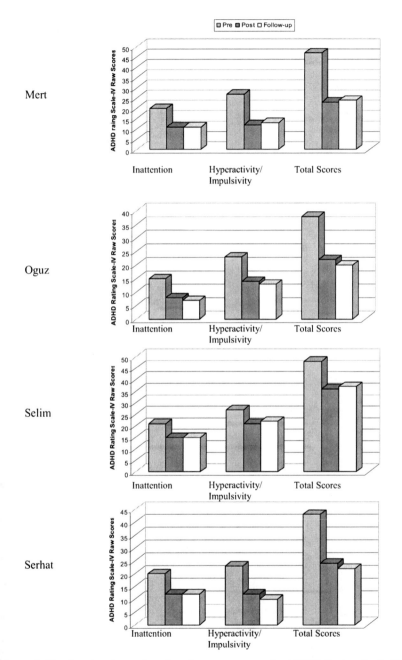

Figure 3. Teachers' ratings of students' raw scores on the ADHD Rating Scale-IV.
Observation Results

100

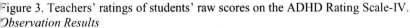

Student academic engagement behaviors were observed trough students' on-task and off-task behaviors. A time-sampling technique (Kerr & Nelson, 1989) was used to record the students' behavior during instructional periods. The observation system involved three categories of behavior: on-task; off-task, active; and off-task, passive. For the descriptions of the behaviors included under each code please refer to the chapter III, the method, on page 83.

Mert.

During baseline, Mert's on-task behaviors were low, ranging from 4 to 8 with a mean of 6.2 (SD=1.48), whereas his off-task-active behaviors was very high ranging from 19 to 23 with a mean of 21.6 (SD=1.52) and his off-task passive behaviors was low ranging from 2 to 4 with a mean of 2.2 (SD=1.48).

With the introduction of the FSS program, Mert's on-task behaviors immediately increased, whereas his off-task active behaviors significantly decreased. Mert's on-task behaviors remained very high, ranging from 18 to 26 with a mean of 23.57 (SD=1.67), and off-task active behaviors stayed low ranging from 1 to 7 with a mean of 4.47 (SD=1.65). Mert's off-task passive behaviors also remained low ranging from 0 to 4 with a mean of 1.63 (SD=1.27). It should be noted that, however, Mert's off-task active behaviors raised significantly during the transitions when the entire class is noisy and behavior expectations were not clear.

During follow-up phase, Mert's on-task behaviors remained high ranging from 20 to 24 with a mean of 22 (SD=1.63) whereas his off-task behaviors stayed low ranging from 3 to 7 with a mean of 5 (SD=1.53). In addition, his off-task passive behaviors stayed low ranging from 0 to 4 with a mean of 3 (SD=1.41). In sum, the FSS program resulted in substantially increased levels of on-task behavior and decreased levels of off-task active behavior for Mert.

Table 9

Mert's Mean, SD, and Range scores on the Academic Engagement Time Observations

	Baseline			Intervention			Follow up		
	Mean	SD	Range	Mean	SD	Range	Mean	SD	Range
On-task	6.2	1.48	4-8	23.47	1.7	18-26	22	1.63	20-24
Off-task active	21.6	1.52	19-23	4.47	1.66	1-7	5	1.53	3-7
Off-task passive	1.48	2.2	2-4	1.63	1.27	0-4	3	1.41	3-4

Oguz.

During baseline, Oguz's on-task behaviors was low, ranging from 3 to 9 with a mean of 6 SD=3), whereas his off-task active behaviors was very high ranging from 18 to 27 with a mean of 21.33 (SD=4.9) and his off-task passive behaviors was low ranging from 0 to 5 with a mean of 2.67 (SD=2.52).

As soon as the intervention was introduced, an immediate positive increase in Oguz's on-task behaviors and a significant decrease in off-task-active behaviors were observed. During the intervention phase, Oguz's on-task behaviors remained very high ranging from 18 to 23 with a mean of 20.97, and his percentage of off-task active behaviors was low ranging from 4 to 12 with a mean of 7.96 (SD=2.12). Oguz's off-task passive behaviors also remained low ranging from 0 to 4 with a mean of 1.03 (SD=0.96). It should be noted, however, Oguz's off-task active behaviors raised significantly during the transitions where behavior expectations were not clear and when the entire class is noisy.

During the follow-up phase, Oguz's on-task behaviors remained high, ranging from 20 to 24 with a mean of 22 (SD=1.63) whereas his off-task active behaviors stayed low ranging from 3 to 7 with a mean of 13.3 (SD=1.53). In addition, his off-task passive behaviors stayed low ranging from 0 to 4 with a mean of 3 (SD=3.7). In sum, the FSS program resulted in substantially increased levels of on-task behavior and decreased levels of off-task active behavior for Oguz.

Table 10

Oguz's Mean, SD, and Range scores on the Academic Engagement Time Observations

	Baseline			Intervention			Follow up		
	Mean	SD	Range	Mean	SD	Range	Mean	SD	Range
On-task	6	3	3-9	20.97	1.71	18-23	22	1.63	20-24
Off-task active	21.33	4.93	18-27	7.97	2.12	4-12	5	1.53	3-7
Off-task passive	2.66	2.51	0-5	1.03	0.96	0-4	3	1.41	0-4

Selim.

During baseline, Selim's on-task behaviors were low, ranging from 8 to 16, with a mean of 11.46 (SD=2.14), whereas his off-task active behaviors were very high, ranging from 13 to 17 with a mean of 14.54 (SD=3.7) and his off-task-passive behaviors was low ranging from 0 to 8 with a mean of 3.78 (SD=2.04).

As soon as the intervention was initiated, an immediate positive increase in Selim's on-task behaviors and a significant decrease in off-task active behaviors were observed. During the intervention phase, Selim's on-task behaviors remained very high ranging from 23 to 27 with a mean of 25.27 (SD=0.98), and his percentage of off-task active behaviors was low ranging from 2 to 7 with a mean of 4 (SD=1.44). Selim's off- task passive behaviors also remained low ranging from 0 to 3 with a mean of 0.8 (SD=0.92). It should be noted that, however, Selim's off-task active behaviors increased during the transitions when most of his classmates were all around the classroom and behavior expectations were not clear.

During follow-up phase, Selim's on-task behaviors remained high ranging from 20 to 23 with a mean of 21.86 (SD=1.07) whereas his off-task behaviors stayed low ranging from 4 to 7 with a mean of 5.43 (SD=0.97). In addition, his off-task passive behaviors stayed low ranging from 0 to 5 with a mean of 2.71 (SD=1.38). In sum, the FSS program resulted in substantially increased levels of on-task behavior and decreased levels of off-task active behavior for Selim.

Table 11

Selim's Mean, SD, and Range scores on the Academic Engagement Time Observations

	Baseline			Intervention			Follow up		
	Mean	SD	Range	Mean	SD	Range	Mean	SD	Range
On-task	11.46	2.14	8-16	25.27	0.98	23-27	21.86	1.07	20-23
Off-task active	14.54	3.71	11-17	4	1.14	2-7	5.43	0.98	4-7
Off-task passive	3.79	2.04	0-8	0.8	0.92	0-3	2.71	1.38	1-5

Serhat.

During baseline, Serhat's on-task behaviors was low ranging from 3 to 9 with a mean of 6 (SD=3), whereas his off-task-active behaviors was very high ranging from 18 to 27 with a mean of 21.33 (SD=4.93) and his off-task-passive behaviors was low ranging from 0 to 5 with a mean of 2.67 (SD=2.52).

As soon as the intervention was introduced, an immediate positive increase in Serhat's on-task behaviors and a significant decrease in off-task-active behaviors were observed. During the intervention phase, Serhat's on-task behaviors remained very high ranging from 18 to 23 with a mean of 20.97 (SD=1.71), and his percentage of off-task- active behaviors was low ranging from 4 to 12 with a mean of 7.96 (SD=2.12). Serhat's off-task-passive behaviors also remained low ranging from 0 to 4 with a mean of 1.03 (SD=0.96). It should be noted that, however, Serhat's off-task-active behaviors rose during transitions when the entire class is noisy and behavior expectations were not clear.

During follow-up phase, Serhat's on-task behaviors remained high ranging from 20 to 24 with a mean of 22 (SD=1.63) whereas his off-task behaviors stayed low ranging from 3 to 7 with a mean of 5 (SD=1.53). In addition, his off-task-passive behaviors stayed low ranging from 0 to 4 with a mean of 3 (SD=1.41). In sum, the FSS program resulted in substantially increased levels of on-task behavior and decreased levels of off-task active behavior for Serhat.

Table 12

Serhat's Mean, SD, and Range scores on the Academic Engagement Time Observations

	Baseline			Intervention			Follow up		
	Mean	SD	Range	Mean	SD	Range	Mean	SD	Range
On-task	13	2.21	18-10	22.67	1.81	20-26	21.29	1.7	18-23
Off-task active	15.67	2.31	12-19	6.97	1.63	4-10	7	1.41	4-8
Off-task passive	1.25	1.48	0-4	0.37	1.61	0-2	1.71	1.38	0-4

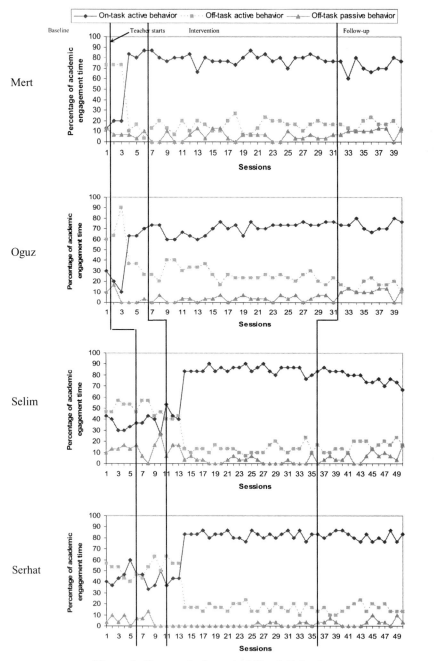

Figure 4. Changes in On-task/Off-task Behaviors.

Effectiveness oj the PSS Program on Class-wide Student Behaviors and Teacher Behaviors

The effectiveness of the FSS program and its impact on class-wide student behaviors and teacher behaviors was evaluated by comparing pre and post intervention scores on the Teacher Ratings of Behavior. The Teacher Ratings of Behavior is a 4-point Likert type scale and translated into Turkish by the researcher. Participant teachers were asked to complete the questionere twice; before the intervention and after the intervention.

The Results of Teacher Ratings of Class-Wide Student Behaviors

Teachers' test scores on the Teacher Ratings of Behavior showed that all participant teachers reported positive changes on class-wide student behaviors. Although teachers' some of the preintervention scores remained same after the intervention, there were positive changes on most items.

Table 13

Teachers' Pre and Post Ratings of the Class-wide Student Behaviors

Generally, how often does YOUR CLASSROOM as a whole	Teacher 1		Teacher 2		Teacher 3		Teacher 4	
	Pre	Post	Pre	Post	Pre	Post	Pre	Post
Behave appropriately in nonclassroom settings (restroom, hallway, lunchroom, playground), e.g., walks quietly, follow directions and rules, etc.	2	2	2	3	2	3	2	3
Follow classroom rules	2	4	3	4	3	3	3	3
Listen to and follow directions	2	4	3	4	3	3	3	3
Behave during "free times"	1	2	2	3	2	3	2	3
Stay engaged in activities/display good work habits	2	3	3	4	3	3	3	4
Raise hands before talking	3	4	3	4	3	3	2	3
Line up appropriately	3	4	3	4	2	2	2	3
Behave well during transitions	2	3	2	3	2	2	2	3
Seek teacher attention at appropriate times	2	3	3	3	3	3	2	3
Interact appropriately with each other	2	3	3	3	3	3	2	3
Comply with teacher requests	2	4	3	4	3	4	3	4
Cooperate and share with each other	2	3	3	3	3	3	3	3
Talk during inappropriate times	2	1	3	2	3	2	3	2
React with defiance to instructions or commands	1	0	0	0	1	0	1	0

Note. 0: Never; 1: Seldom; 2: Occasionally; 3: Usually; 4: Always

The Results of Teacher Ratings of Teacher Behaviors

The results of teacher ratings of teacher behaviors showed that there were dramatic changes on all participant teachers' pre- and post-test scores for teacher behaviors. As seen in Table 14, all participant teachers reported difficulty in being able to find opportunities to focus on appropriate behavior by praising children. The teachers also reported that they were experiencing significant problems in their classrooms through spending a lot of time focusing on the inappropriate behavior of just few children, feeling like spending more time correcting inappropriate behavior rather than teaching, and constantly having to reprimand children for inappropriate behavior. Post intervention ratings of the teachers reflected dramatic changes on these items. Only item 2, having a hard time implementing quick and smooth transitions, remained the same for Teachers 2 and 4 after the intervention.

Overall results showed that the FSS program was effective on improving the teachers' classroom management skills. Teachers reported that they were able to find more opportunities to focus on appropriate behavior by praising children. Additionally, teachers reported that they spent less time focusing on the inappropriate behavior of just a few children and less felt like they spent more time correcting inappropriate behavior rather than teaching.

Table 14

Teachers' Pre and Post Ratings of the Teacher Behaviors

Generally, do you feel as a <u>TEACHER</u> that you	Teacher 1		Teacher 2		Teacher 3		Teacher 4	
	<u>Pre</u>	<u>Post</u>	<u>Pre</u>	<u>Post</u>	<u>Pre</u>	<u>Post</u>	<u>Pre</u>	<u>Post</u>
Spend a lot of time focusing on the inappropriate behavior of just a few children	4	1	3	1	4	1	3	1
Have a hard time implementing quick and smooth transitions	3	2	2	2	3	2	2	2
Constantly have to reprimand children for inappropriate behavior	4	1	4	1	3	1	3	1
Are able to find opportunities to focus on appropriate behavior by praising children	2	4	1	3	2	4	1	3
Feel like you spend more time correcting inappropriate behavior rather than teaching	3	1	4	1	4	1	3	1

Note. 0: Never; 1: Seldom; 2: Occasionally; 3: Usually; 4: Always

The Reactions/Opinions of Participant Teachers and Parents

Regarding the FSS Program

The opinions of participant teachers and parents were explored on a range of issues relating to the effectiveness of the FSS program. Semi-structured interviews were carried out with the teachers and parents in order to obtain in-dept information on the following topics: the success of the FSS program, the use of the FSS program, what teachers/parents liked most and least about the FSS program, cultural barriers to the success of the program, and recommendations to the program.

All participant teachers except teacher 3 stated that they found the FSS program very successful and liked many aspects of the program. In particular, the teachers expressed a strong belief on the necessity of active parent involvement in children's education. They further explained that they liked the parent education module the most about the FSS program as the module facilitated active parental involvement. On the other hand, a common concern expressed by the teachers was that the teachers had difficulty finding the time needed for each participant child in order to implement the program

Teacher 1 said that the FSS program was effective in reducing Mert's problem behaviors. Further, she explained that the program resulted in improved social skills, and academic achievement for Mert. The program also helped Teacher 1 and Mert's family to establish close communication. When asked to comment on the success of the FSS program for Oguz, Teacher 2 explained that:

I was skeptical initially that Oguz's family would not commit to such program. But I have been pleasantly surprised and enthused by the changes to their working practice which we have made working together, sharing information and implementing FSS with Oguz. I think the FSS program was clearly beneficial for Oguz and in general this is manifested trough improved attendance, more positive attitude toward school, and I guess in short, better behavior.

Teacher 3 found that the FSS program was effective to some extent, but could not achieve its intended goals entirely because there was no collaboration between Selim's parents and herself. She stated "It is so sad to see that parents are more protective of their children even when they are wrong" Teacher 3 explained that:

Though we come a long way with Selim in all areas, he is still difficult at school. I feel

that I am alone in teaching him to behave at school and still struggle at times. I have tried

everything that has been suggested me. He has made progress, but that is not enough. I

know that there is more he could do if he had the desire, but he doesn't. He spends most

of his energy avoiding anything and everything that may pose a challenge. He is also so

unpredictable. Sometimes he really cooperates with me, follow my directions, and tries

so hard to do the tasks that I give him, but sometimes whatever I do, he is being mean to

other children and does not follow my directions. I do not have any clue what is going on

his home. I know that his family struggles with many issues. I think the problems at home

make it very difficult for him to adjust to the school.

Teacher 4 found the program very successful with Student 4, Serhat. Teacher 4 explained

that;

There is a marked improvement in Serhat's self-confidence. His social skills improved

and he became less argumentative. It has been amazing to see that his attitude towards

his learning has been transformed. He has greater concentration, self confidence,

improved self-expression, and better behavior. His family was very supportive of his

progress and worked so hard to help him to learn to control his anger and also enjoy his

success with the FSS program.

The Use of the FSS Program

All participant teachers agreed that the implementing the FSS program with the use of red

and green card was very easy and effective. The teacher 4 said that "Using a visual cue as a

prompt and also as a reminder helped Serhat to maximize his on-task behaviors. That was much

more effective than anything I did before." The teachers also agreed that the rewarding the target child when the target child reaches his daily goals was very easy to do. Teacher 2 emphasized that rewarding the whole class worked really well in her classroom. She stated that:

Rewarding my whole class was the part that I liked most about the FSS program. This system fostered each of my student's care for the success of the target child and motivated meaningful group cooperation. I mean, not only the target child, but also my entire class became motivated to behave appropriately."

In addition, Teachers 1, 2, and 4 also reported that they did not have any difficulty in maintaining communication with parents by using the daily report cards. Only Teacher 3 reported problems regarding communicating with the target child's parents.

Although in general all teachers found the FSS program easy to use, they also reported that they had difficulty finding the time to implement the program particularly when the implementation time span became longer. Teacher 1 said that:

The program was so easy to use in the beginning. Then the implementation took longer and longer towards the end of the intervention. There were many times that I found it so hard to continue showing the red and green card because I was in the middle of a lesson. There were also times when the entire class was noisy and at times when the class became unmanageable, I felt that it was unfair to expect from my target child to behave appropriately. But I managed to keep continue and as a result, Mert gained progressively greater levels of control, awareness, and self-esteem. I felt that it was worth putting so much effort on it.

What Teachers Liked Most and Least About the FSS Program?

Teacher 1, 2 and 4 stated that what they liked most about the FSS program was the parent

114

training module. Teacher 4 said that "I think when a child acts out at school there are always some reasons behind it. In my experience, most reasons come from families. There can be lack of parental supervision, use of corporal punishment, sometimes high family conflict or you know other issues. I talked to Mert's parents about Mert's behaviors once and next day I learned that Mert was beaten up by his father really badly. I certainly do not agree with their way to discipline Mert. Because you know they are being role models for him. But I also do not want to be on the opposite sides of them. Because I think that once you break the ropes with parents, that just worsen the problems. So in these kinds of situations, I always feel that I need a mediator between me and the child's parents, someone who can teach parents the right way to help their child. FSS coach provided Mert's family with necessary education that they needed to support Mert's success at school."

Teacher 2 stated that:

When you try to help a student and the parents refuse all sources of help, it's frustrating, demanding, and exhausting. But if you know that parents also invest their time and energy to help their child, then it becomes worth the effort, the worry, the frustration, and the stress to be here. Because you know that your effort will soon make a difference in your student's life. Therefore, I liked the parents education module as the best. I think that the program helps parents to understand their influence on their children's education and most importantly it provides them with practical skills and strategies for effectively managing problem behaviors.

Teacher 3 addressed that what she liked the most about the FSS program was the program's emphasize on positive behaviors. She stated that she was not used to tell students what they are doing correctly and praise them for appropriate behaviors. Instead she made it clear that

115

she did not approve by calling out students' names and reminding them they misbehaved. Teacher 3 also stated that she was not aware of her need to improve her methods of handling difficult behaviors in the classroom with positive results before she entered into the program. She expressed that:

> After I began using positive behavior management techniques, I recognized the importance of praise. Serhat became responsive to my praise and showed some progress in following classroom rules, paying attention to activities, and interacting with his peers in a more friendly way to some extent. I think that this is a real success for Selim, although his behavior is unpredictable at times. I can tell you honestly that some of the things that I hear that going on at home, you are just amazed by it, and you think how can a child come in here and learn when they are dealing with all these issues at home? Especially when there is abuse going on at home.

When asked about what they liked least about the program, all teachers agreed that the program required a great deal of teacher time spent on intervening rather than instruction. Participant teachers stated that they each had a very large class with 40 or 44 students and most students need individualized attention. Teacher 2 said that:

> The problems always get worse in the 1st grade. Most kids in my classroom did not go to kindergarten at all. As you know kindergarten is an important transitional phase for the kids to get used to regular school environment. Therefore, in general most kids in the first grade do not know what to do, what to expect, or how to behave. School is their first experience to stay seated and listen to someone for a long period of time. So, I am accustomed to see the first graders all over the classroom for the first couple of months. Then, they progressively learn to sit down and listen quietly. Overall, first grade is really

challenging for a teacher. You have to teach a lot to the kids not only reading and writing but also many other stuff too. So when you think about what we have to deal in the first grade then you realize that every extra thing, such as implementing FSS, adds so much stress on teachers. In my situation, I really wanted to be a part of the FSS program and your study. However, I am not sure whether other teachers would be willing to be a part of the program. I think that they would be skeptical about the heavy time commitment required in the program.

Cultural Barriers to the Success of the Program

Teacher 3 explained that:

There are some general things that I consider as barriers to the success of such programs. For example, most of our parents are not actively involved in their children's education. When you talk to parents about the importance education, they will tell you 'Oh, I will fully support my child attend school as long as she wishes to continue education.' Unfortunately most parents do not recognize that this is not something that you can leave to your child to decide. It is parents' responsibility to help their child with homework and studying. You have to motivate the kid to be successful at school. It is not something that you can leave it to chance.

Teacher 1 shared very similar ideas with Teacher 3:

A child who does not believe that academic success is important will not work for it. A child who does not believe that he can be successful in school won't make a consistent effort to do well at school. If parents want their children to be successful at school they must help them understand the value and importance of academic achievement. I think in general parents' lack of school involvement and lack of concern for their children's education is very significant in my classroom. Parents have a crucial role in their child's education. Therefore, parental education is necessary particularly for my underachiever students. However, I already have an excessive workload. Personally, I feel I could not take on another role even so I would not feel comfortable within this role. FSS program takes kind of responsibility at that point. The program coach educates parents and recruits them as partners with the school.

Teacher 4 also underlined a different problem as a potential cultural barrier.

I think in Serhat's case his parents are over-involved with him. Not just his parents but his grandparents as well. His parents have not encouraged him to be self-sufficient and have not taught him the skills of effort and responsibility. I guess whenever they try; the grandparents always interfere negatively with their different parenting style. His grandparents are too helpful and overprotective. Basically Serhat is confused about how to behave appropriately and to do well at school. That is one of the major problems that I see in the children of extended families. Most of these children like Serhat do not have consistency and structure at home to learn necessary skills to do well socially and academically.

Recommendations to the Program

When asked whether teachers have any recommendations to the FSS program, all teachers shared their point of views on the FSS program. "One of the things I learned from being involved in the FSS program is that my learning is never done." Teacher 1 said.

I have to consistently update my knowledge and skills. Joining the FSS program provided me with an opportunity to learn more about positive behavior management. It is such a simple concept that is easily implemented yet yields incredible results. I know it is hard for some to believe that these changes can really occur this quickly. Once you start, you realize all anyone really wants is to have someone believe in them. I do not have any recommendations to the program but I do recommend this program to any teacher who struggles with problem behaviors.

Teacher 2 stated that:

In my idea, the key of FSS program is self-management rather than child management-to always be aware of where and how I use my energy, so I'm always looking for opportunities to recognize what is happening positively or the absence of the negative things. The program allows me to stay on the positive side of my students' behavior... It is really good to implement such an uplifting and energizing program especially if you worry about burn-out, and losing effectiveness. I would strongly recommend this program to all my colleagues.

Teacher 3 expressed that:

It was so great to be able to get a professional's insight into what was happening from a more objective perspective. Creating change on the problems that go much deeper than just the behaviors is really difficult. I know that such problems do not change over night. It takes time and commitment. I really think that I have changed a lot with the FSS program. I will continue to use consistent, positive reinforcement with Selim. I've learned that using this approach is a process and can't be rushed. I still have some days I feel that we've totally regressed to the old ways. However, for the most part though, my approach is changed forever, I will do my best in order to help Selim. My only suggestion would be continue working with families for much longer time. Not just couple of months.

Teachers 4 stated that:

I have found the FSS program to be extremely effective in my role as a teacher, in my

role as a mother, and in general, in any relationship I have with a child. I highly

recommend the program to any teacher in order to experience a true transformation.

The Reactions/Opinions of Participant Parents Regarding the FSS Program

The Success of the FSS Program

Interviews with parents were conducted at the end of the intervention in order to address

whether the FSS program accomplished its desired effect or not. Parents also addressed their

experiences and views of the FSS program.

All parents shared the similar opinions on the effects of the FSS program on their

children. For example, Parent 1 stated that:

The program helped me to understand what my son was going through and what

challenges he encounters each day. The coach thought me how to handle difficult

situations. She came out every week really bonded with the whole family. She wasn't just

here for Mert. She talked to my husband and I and our other children. She really helped

the whole family. She has been very helpful and supportive. We look forward to seeing

her when she comes out. We learn a lot about what we can do to help Mert. She helped us

by giving ideas on how to increase his attention and help to him with his homework. I am

less angry, less frustrated and less confused. Mert is also less tense, hyper. He spends his

energy in a more constructive way. My husband and I talk to him rather than yelling at

him or spanking him when he does something wrong. He treats his sisters really nicely. I

think that is because he feels that we really love him and appreciate him for his good behaviors.

Parent 2 expressed that:

It has been an amazingly positive experience. The most beneficial part was that the program coach helped me understand the problems we were dealing with and enabled me to deal with it better emotionally. The program has helped us along the way to identify our weaknesses to build on and how to react differently to Oguz's problem behaviors. The coach gave us activities to do with our son to get him where he is now. She gave us lots of ideas and encouragement. I like the program because I can see how my son benefited at school; he is well adapted to the school now.

Parent 3 stated that:

The coach worked with us in the home. She told us how to help my son with his problems at school and home. She would come to our house and talk with me, show me things to do. Overall, she made me feel like she really cared about my family. She has helped me with doctors; where to take my other son. She has supported me a lot. I am very thankful. It is a very good program.

Parent 4 expressed that:

I do not know how we would've made it without the program. I have seen a noticeable difference in my child's behavior in a very short time period. I would recommend the FSS program to anyone. I wish it was available to all children. As a teacher, I see children in the school system that needs professional help. The program coach was so helpful. I never felt put down or judged. She always encouraged me and kept me motivated. She talked to my mother-in-law and father-in-law in order to help them

121

understand my son's needs and try to deal with what is going on. I knew I could always call her about any questions I had. The most beneficial part was that the coach put me at ease and taught me how to help my son deal with his anger and overcome difficulties he is experiencing at school. I know things won't change overnight. But I have already seen so much improvement in my son's behavior. His school work has dramatically improved, he stays focused during homework, and he is less hyper.

The Use of the HomeBase

When asked about whether the program (HomeBase) was easy or hard to use, all parents, except parent 3, agreed that the program (HomeBase) was easy to use. Parent 1, 2, and 4 stated that they received daily feedback about how their son's day went and spent some extra time with their child at a fun activity such as playing a game. Parent expressed that the program provided a great deal of suggestions as far as things that they could do on a daily basis that were really easy to do. Only Parent 3, reported difficulty in understanding some activities and finding extra time to spend with his child.

What Parents Liked Most and Least About the Program

When asked parents what they liked most and least about the program, Parents 1, 3 and 4 stated that they liked the program as a whole and Parent 2 expressed that she liked the Class module most. Parent 1 stated that:

We liked the HomeBase along with the Class. Both worked really well with our son. The program gave us lots of insight as to why our child did what he did, so that we could better help him. It also gave ways to get closer to our son. As a result, not jus our child's behavior improved but also the program made us feel good about the way we parent.

122

Parent 2 expressed that:

Before the program, I strongly believed that my son's teacher failed to make an effort to help my son be successful at school. But now with the help of the FSS program, we understand our part in our son's problem behaviors. Now my husband and I really try to spend quality time with Oguz with different daily activities requested by the program. My son knows that we really appreciate him when he is good at school. When he misbehaves we are not standing behind him anymore. I think that now Oguz knows what is good and bad. He is not confused anymore. Overall, I am amazed at how my son changed for the better. He is succeeding in school and feels a self-confidence he had not felt before. It shows in the way he looks and the way he acts. He tells me all about the great grades he is getting and how he was able to skip ahead in some subjects. He is not the kid who was the problem child anymore. My son is much happier. I cannot say how happy I am to have found a program where my son is encouraged to be successful.

Parents 3 said that:

It is a good program. You are taking care of my son at school. May Allah bless you. I have 7 children and my husband has not had a job for almost three months. I can not even buy a gum for Selim. There are some older children in our neighborhood who steals money from others. I told Selim not to play with them so many times. He did not listen to me and learned many bad things from them. But now he does not play with those children. He studies at home. He even helps me with household chores. All of these are result of the program. He loves you coming our apartment and showing us activities to play with him. We all love you. Selim promised me that he will study so hard and will send you his grades at the end of the year. He tells me that he wants to be a doctor. He would not be like this, if he did not join the FSS program.

Parent 4 expressed that:

I am very satisfied with all aspects of the program. The program helped to build my

child's confidence. Serhat began displaying self control when he gets angry. I think it is

because now he understands the consequences of his behavior. His grades improved and

he really gets along well with his friends.

When asked about what parents liked least about the program, Parent 2 stated that she

had difficulty finding time to do daily activities and Parent 3 expressed that she had difficulty in

understanding some of the activities.

Cultural Barriers to the Success of the Program

When asked about potential cultural barriers to the success of the FSS program parents

expressed their opinions and concerns on some cultural values and attitudes towards education.

Parent 1 stated that:

Whenever I go to school and talk to my son's teacher about my son, I feel so bad about

my parenting. Because, I only get complaints about my son. When I join teacher parent

conferences, I keep quiet. Parents who have better education talk and I listen to them. I

feel like the teacher only gives importance to those parents' ideas. She never asks me for

my ideas. I really feel like there is an intolerable discrimination here, at my son's school.

I mean not just at school, everywhere. People who have more education and money are

more valued than us.

Parent 3 stated that:

Back then it was embarrassing and shameful to educate a girl in the town where I came from. I learned to read and write from my uncle. But I do not know how to help my son since I did not go to school at all. My husband also experienced failure in school. I think, therefore he does not understand the benefits of education. He does not even listen to me when I try to speak to him about the value of education. Now you are helping my son. But what will happen to Selim when the FSS program finishes? We need someone who can help him when you are not here as well.

Parent 4 addressed that:

My mother-in-law and father-in-law live with us and we have daily issues with disciplining my two children. I have different ideas about raising children than my husband's mother and father do. However, in our family the grandparents have just as much of a right to make decisions about raising the children than the parents do. They feel disrespected if I ask them not to do something. Even when I say no to eating junk even minutes before dinner time. So it is so hard for me to prevent my children from spoiling. But now we can better deal with the problems with the help of the FSS program However I am still concerned about what is going to happen in the future when new problems arise.

Parent 2 did not find any cultural barriers to the success of the FSS program.

Recommendations to the FSS Program

All parents recommended that HomeBase should be extended and consultation services for future problems should be provided. Parents also agreed that their children and themselves benefited from the program extensively and they would recommend the program to all other parents.

Social Validity

The Social validity of the FSS program was assessed via a 13-item Likert-type questionere administered to participant teachers and parents at the end of the program.

The participant teachers' responses on the Social validity survey revealed that although all teachers reported high levels of satisfaction with the FSS program, they disagreed on some items. All teachers disagreed on the items, four and five. Specifically, the teachers thought that the program took much of their time and interfered with their other teaching activities/responsibilities. In addition, Teachers 1, 2, and 3 also disagreed concerning ease of the FSS program to use. Teacher 3 reported that she was not satisfied with the change in behavior with her student. On the contrary, she agreed that she noticed change her student's behavior quickly.

As seen in Table 16, all participant parents reported high levels of satisfaction with the FSS program. Only parent 3 disagreed on the program's easiness to use and Parent 2 disagreed on the issue regarding the time that they spent on the program.

126

Table 15

Social Validity/Teacher Satisfaction

	1 Strongly disagree	2 Disagree	3 No opinion	4 Agree	5 Strongly agree
1. The goal of the program fit well with my goals to improve classroom behavior.					T1, T2, T3, T4
2. The goal of the program was compatible with my needs in the classroom.			T2		T1,T3, T4
3. The program was easy to use.		T1, T2, T3,		T4	
4. The program did not take much of my time.		T1, T2, T3, T4			
5. The program did not interfere with my other teaching activities/ responsibilities.		T1, T2, T3, T4			
6. I am satisfied with the change in behavior with my student.		T3			T1, T2, T4
7. I noticed changes in my student's behavior quickly.				T3	T1, T2, T4
8. The program was effective in teaching my student appropriate behavior.			T3		T1, T2, T4
9. The program had a positive effect on the target child's peer relationships.				T3	T1, T2, T4
10. I received adequate training to use the program.					T1, T2, T3, T4
11. I received on-going support/help while using the program.					T1, T2, T3, T4
12. I would recommend the program to other teachers.					T1, T2, T3, T4
13. I would use the program with other students in the future.					T1, T2, T3, T4

Note. T1: Teacher 1; T2: Teacher 2; T3: Teacher 3; T4: Teacher 4

Table 16

Social Validity/Parent Satisfaction

	1 Strongly disagree	2 Disagree	3 No opinion	4 Agree	5 Strongly agree
1. The goal of the program fit well with my goals to improve home behavior of my child.					P1, P2, P3, P4
2. The goal of the program was compatible with my needs at home.				P1	P2, P3, P4
3. The program was easy to use.		P3		P2	P1, P4
4. The program did not take much of my time.		P2		P1, P3, P4	
5. The program did not interfere with my other activities/ responsibilities at home.				P1, P2, P3	P4
6. I am satisfied with the change in behavior with my child.				P3	P1, P2, P4
7. I noticed changes in my child's behavior quickly.					P1, P2, P3, P4
8. The program was effective in teaching my child appropriate behavior.				P3	P1, P2, P4
9. The program had a positive effect on my child's peer relationships.					P1, P2, P3, P4
10. I received adequate training to use the program.					P1, P2, P3, P4
11. I received on-going support/help while using the program.					P1, P2, P3, P4
12. I would recommend the program to other parents.					P1, P2, P3, P4

Note. P1: Parent 1; P2: Parent 2; P3: Parents 3; P4: Parent 4

CHAPTER V

Discussion

Statement of Purpose

In this study, the effectiveness of the First Step to Success early intervention program on Turkish children with AD/HD and perceptions of participant Turkish teachers and parents in regard to the FSS program were investigated. In order to examine the effectiveness of the First Step to Success program, (1) participant children's social and emotional problems, (2) participant children's problem behaviors, (3) class-wide student behaviors, (4) teacher behaviors, and (5) perceptions of the participant Turkish teachers and parents in regard to the FSS program were explored. A multiple baseline study was conducted across two groups of children with AD/HD including two first grade students each.

1. Participant children's social emotional problems were measured with Child Behavior Checklist (at baseline, before and after the intervention) and TRF (at baseline, before and after the intervention).

2. Participant children's problem behaviors were evaluated using ADHD Rating Scale-IV (at baseline, before and after the intervention) and observational data (at baseline, during and after the intervention).

3. Class-wide student behaviors were measured using the Teacher Ratings of Behavior (before and after intervention).

4. Teacher behaviors were evaluated using Teachers Ratings of Teacher Behavior (before and after intervention).

5. The perceptions of the participant Turkish teachers and parents in regard to the FSS program were explored with the semi-structured interviews.

Summary and Discussion

Attention-deficit/hyperactivity disorder (AD/HD) is a diagnostic label given to children who have significant deficiencies in sustained attention, organization, impulse control, and the regulation of activity level in response to situational demands (Barkley, 1989). As a result of these deficiencies, children with AD/HD experience severe pervasive impairment in several areas of development including social relationships, academic progress, and self-esteem. The difficulties in childhood extend into adolescence and adulthood, and are predictive of more serious problems later in life.

Within the medical and educational communities, a diverse range of viewpoints exists on treatment and interventions for children AD/HD. A relatively new, and encouraging, approach to children with social and behavioral problems is the First Step to Success program. The First Step to Success is an early intervention program designed to address the needs of young children identified as being at-risk for developing or having anti-social or aggressive behaviors. This early intervention program achieves secondary prevention goals by recruiting parents as partners with the school in teaching the at-risk children a behavior pattern contributing to school success and the development of friendships. Research demonstrated that the FSS program produces robust treatment effects for the majority of at-risk children to whom it is applied (Diken & Rutherford, 2005; Walket et al., 1998).

When the First Step to Success program is used for children with AD/HD, it may promote meaningful improvement in children's challenging behavior through its' strong components, the CLASS and the HomeBase. These two components of the program focus on problematic social behaviors and disrupting classroom behaviors as well as social skills and social performance deficits of targeted children. In addition, the FSS program facilitates the behavioral changes in a cross situational fashion both at home and school.

A careful review of the available literature suggests that children with AD/HD show performance deficits rather than a skill deficit (Maedgen & Carlson, 2000). Social performance deficits are more difficult to ameliorate than skills deficits for many reasons. First, most currently available social skills trainings (SST) target deficits in skills rather than deficits in performance. Second, because social performance problems occur across settings (e.g., classroom, playground, home, neighborhood), interventions addressing these difficulties must be implemented by a variety of individuals in a cross-situational fashion (DuPaul, 2003). Third, most SST programs do not consider the unique topography of each child's performance in the social domain. In other words, pretreatment assessment data may not have been gathered to clarify the specific needs of each treated child, thus leading to a poor fit between presenting problems and SST objectives (Landau & Milich, 1998). Finally, research shows that the disrupting classroom behaviors of children with AD/HD also contribute to their social problems (Erhardt & Hinshaw, 1994; Pelham & Bender, 1982). Therefore, interventions for children with AD/HD should also focus on decreasing children's disturbing classroom behaviors as much as their negative social behaviors.

The present study investigated the efficacy of the First Step to Success program on social-emotional problems and problem behaviors of Turkish children with AD/HD. Three reasons highlight the importance of this study.

First, this study is the first to evaluate the efficacy of the FSS program with Turkish children with AD/HD in Turkey. Indeed, it is the only study to investigate the efficacy of a multicomponent intervention program with Turkish children with AD/HD in Turkey. Emerging studies conducted in Turkey are mostly on the effects of parent training programs on the problem behaviors of Turkish children with AD/HD (Erman, 2001).

Second, the present study is the first to investigate the effectiveness of the FSS program with children with ADHD. Previous studies on the effectiveness of the FSS program were conducted with young children who developed emerging signs of antisocial behavior patterns.

Third, although the FSS program implemented under challenging circumstances in Turkey, (in large classrooms with 40 to 43 children in each classroom), findings demonstrated significant gains in academic engagement behavior, diminished social emotional problems, and diminished problem behaviors of all Turkish children with AD/HD.

Overall, this is an important study that makes significant contribution to establishing an effective intervention option for children with AD/HD. The result of the study on participant children's social emotional problems and problem behaviors, limitations, implications for practice, and implications for future research are discussed in the following section.

Discussion

Effectiveness of the FSS Program on Participant Children's Problem Behaviors

The effectiveness of the FSS program on participant children's problem behaviors were examined by direct observations of on-task behaviors and teacher ratings on the ADHD Rating Scale-IV. Direct observations indicated that with the introduction of the FSS program, all participant children's on-task behaviors immediately increased, whereas their off-task active behaviors significantly decreased. At the end of the FSS program, participant children's on task

132

behaviors remained high and their off-task active behaviors continued to occur at low levels. Follow-up observation results at three months, also indicated that the FSS program resulted in substantially increased levels of on-task behavior and decreased levels of off-task active behavior for all participant children. It should be noted, however, that off-task-active behaviors of three children, Oguz, Selim, and Serhat raised significantly during the transitions where behavior expectations were not clear and when the entire class was noisy.

Teacher ratings on the AD/HD Rating Scale-IV were gathered to examine the effectiveness of the FSS program on AD/HD symptomatology of participant children. As soon as the intervention began, Mert and Serhat's problem behaviors associated to AD/HD were significantly reduced and positive behaviors, such as following directions without being disruptive or aggressive, staying seated, working on-tasks, and participating in class activities, were significantly increased. After the intervention ended, Teacher 1 and Teacher 4's ratings on the AD/HD Rating Scale-IV provided a strong evidence of statistically reliable change in terms of Mert and Serhat's Inattention and Hyperactive-Impulsive symptoms were due to the FSS early intervention program. In addition, Teacher 2's ratings on the AD/HD Rating Scale-IV showed that although there was a little evidence of statistically reliable change in terms of Oguz's Inattention symptoms, the changes on his Hyperactivity-Impulsivity symptoms were due to the FSS program.

Teacher 3's ratings revealed that she did not find the FSS program successful on Selim's AD/HD symtomatology. Although she pointed out some decreases of Selim's AD/HD symptoms, her ratings of Selim's AD/HD symptoms remained in the clinical range. In other words, the decreases of Selim's AD/HD symptoms were not statistically significant; however, the FSS program was successful at least to some extent with Selim.

Teacher 3 overall believed that Selim's problem behaviors were caused by poor parenting and a "chaotic" home environment. She commented that the FSS program helped Selim to some extent but had not been a "cure". Teacher 3 believed that the FSS program would be a short term solution for Selim. For the long term, she thought that both Selim and his family need extensive help from various resources. When asked about the potential negative effects of program infidelity, Teacher 3 stated that she found it difficult to simultaneously teach to the group, monitor Selim's behavior, be consistent with the red/green card, and watch the others' behaviors at the same time. In addition, she expressed that although she acknowledged that positive reinforcement was essential for the program success, it was hard for her to come up with an effective positive reinforcement of good behavior. When Teacher 3 commented on Selim's good behavior, then most of the 43 children in her class started looking for attention from her all at the same time. Finally, Teacher 3 expressed that she became concerned that the program was overshadowing her teaching.

Although positive effects of the FSS program on participant children's problem behaviors were demonstrated by direct observations and Teachers 1, 2, and 4's ratings on the ADHD Rating Scale-IV, the results of direct observations of Selim were not supported by Teacher 3's ratings on the ADHD Rating Scale-IV. Teacher 3 reported a slight decrease of Selim's AD/HD symptomatology, however the results were not statistically significant. These results will be discussed with respect to the results of teacher ratings on participant children's social emotional and behavioral problems.

Effectiveness of the FSS Program on Participant Children's Social and Emotional Problems

The effectiveness of the FSS program on participant children's social and emotional problems was examined by the CBCL and TRF. Preintervention results indicated that participant children were on the clinical or borderline range on both CBCL and TRF. All participant parents' post intervention ratings on the CBCL revealed significant increases on the competence scales and significant decreases on the problem scales. Similarly, teacher ratings on the TRF revealed a significant increase on the Adaptive Functioning scale and significant decreases on the Total Problem scales. Although Teacher 3 reported significant decreases on Selim's symptoms associated with AD/HD, she did not report immediate decreases on Selim's emotional and behavioral behaviors.

All parents reported significant reductions in their children's problem behaviors. Parent ratings on the CBCL indicated significantly lower levels of aggression, as well as lower levels of attention problems, and social problems. Consistent with the parent ratings, Teachers 1, 2, and 4 also reported increased levels of academic engagement time and less problem behaviors in the classroom. More specifically, teacher ratings on the TRF showed significantly lower levels of aggression, as well as attention problems and social problems.

Although similar results were obtained in previous studies conducted on the effectiveness of the FSS program with children with emotional and behavioral problems (Golly, Sprague, & Walker, 2000; Diken & Rutherford, 2005; Lien-Thorne & Kamps, 2005; Overton, McKenzie, & King, 2002), this study was the first to evaluate the effectiveness of the First Step to Success program on children with AD/HD. Thus, findings demonstrate promise for the use of the FSS program with children diagnosed with AD/HD.

Teacher 3 did not report consistent improvements in Selim's problem behaviors and academic performance. When asked about the reasons for the inconsistent behavioral changes, Teacher 3 was quick to comment on the problems at home. She explained that Selim's family was suffering from lack of basic necessities, the difficulties of daily living, stress produced by extreme poverty, and social marginalization as they just moved to Ankara from a small urban town in Eastern part of Turkey. She felt that Selim did not have good conditions for learning because he lacked a special place at home to conduct his studies. His nutrition was poor and had negative effects upon his health. Further, Teacher 3 explained that she met with Selim's parents only once to discuss how to help Selim more effectively but the meeting ended up in an argument over who was to blame. From that time on, misunderstanding and high conflict between Selim's parents and Teacher 3 continued to escalate. As the conflict escalated, it prevented necessary progress in helping Selim to manage his anger and his low academic engagement. When the FSS program was introduced to Teacher 3, she became skeptical about the time commitment required by the program and cooperation between Selim's parents and herself needed to achieve the FSS program goals. Selim's parents were also skeptical about their ability to implement the program. Both sides were convinced that they could overcome the challenges with the help of the program coach. When the program ended, Teacher 3 reported that she noticed some positive changes on Selim's emotional and behavioral problems but the changes were not consistent enough to say that the FSS program was successful with Selim. Teacher 3 argued that the inconsistency of the behavioral changes of Selim was caused by the problems at home. She explained that in her opinion, school has limited influence on children's behaviors. When a child is exposed to extreme family problems such as poverty, lack of supervision, and physical abuse at home, the effects make themselves known as behavioral problems at school. Teacher 3 believed that if the risk factors including familial and environmental risks can not be eliminated in a child's life, than the remediation of the child's emotional and behavioral problems become extremely difficult.

Other reasons for the limited success of the program with Selim might be Teacher 3's implementation of the CLASS and lack of classroom management skills. During the consultant phase, the program coach had difficulty from time to time to determine whether Selim's behavior was "green" or "red." The degree of freedom the class experienced and the frequency of reminders needed to redirect students to their tasks showed that behavioral expectations were not clear in the classroom. Research has shown that poorly managed classrooms have higher levels of classroom aggression and rejection that, in turn, influence the continuing escalation of individual child behavior problems (Kellam, Ling, Merisca, Brown, & Ialongon, 1988). On the other hand, considerable research has also demonstrated that effective classroom management can reduce disruptive behavior and enhance social and academic achievement (Brophy, 1996; Walker et al., 1995). Given the importance of classroom management skills, the program coach provided Teacher 3 with the necessary resources and information on how to make necessary changes to offer an activity that provided more structure and clear expectations and classroom management skills that are associated with improved classroom behavior (e.g., high levels of praise and social reinforcement; ignoring minor problem behaviors, the use of proactive strategies such as preparing for transitions and establishing clear, predictable rules; using short, clear commands, warning, reminders, and distractions effectively; the use of tangible reinforcement systems for appropriate).

In addition, monitoring the program's implementation to immediately deal with any

137

problems that may arise was not possible during the study. Teacher 3 appeared well prepared and comfortable in implementing the green/red card in the beginning of the study. The program coach, however, observed that Teacher 3 forgot to record and award the daily points frequently. Therefore, the coach demonstrated a consistent effort to encourage Teacher 3 to increase her consistency with the rewards and her verbal praise statements as well as to continue to try to reduce her attention to negative behaviors.

Selim's trouble maintaining on-task behavior during the teacher phase might be also because of Teacher 3's routine of providing attention to Selim when he was not doing what he was supposed to do. When the program coach discussed with Teacher 3 the importance of positive reinforcement in teaching, Teacher 3 expressed that she did not want Selim to become dependent upon to praise. The program coach provided Teacher 3 with information that the eventual goal is to shift away from exclusive teacher management to increasing student self-management skills.

Previous studies on the effectiveness of the FSS program showed that the inconsistency in a teacher's implementation would make it difficult for a child to gain momentum (Diken & Rutherford, 2005; Overton, McKenzie, & Reese, 2002). After gaining a momentum, a step by step progress towards self-management skills have the potential for producing more durable and generalizable behavior gains in situations outside the classroom. Teacher 3 also addressed that using the red/green card the entire school day was tiring on her with her excessive workload and other students with challenging behaviors in her classroom.

After the program ended, the teacher ratings on the TRF demonstrated that Selim displayed a significant increase on the Adaptive Functioning scale and had improved slightly on the Total Problem scales while remaining in the clinical range. In particular, Selim's Attention

138

Problems scale score dropped to normal range, whereas, his Aggressive Problems scale score dropped to borderline clinical range.

Although Teacher 3 pointed out that the FSS program did not resulted with consistent behavioral changes for Selim, Parent 3 believed that the FSS program significantly decreased Selim's problem behaviors at home. Selim's mother reported behavioral changes especially on Aggressive Problems and Attention Problems scales on the CBCL. In the interview with her, Parent 3 explained that Selim became less argumentative with her and displayed less aggressive behaviors. When asked about Selim's problem behaviors at school, Parent 3 blamed Teacher 3, saying she had "humiliated" her son so many times in front of the class and caused him not to love school and be disruptive. She also added that Selim's teacher was rude to her on a couple of occasions, made her wait a long time without saying a word.

Selim's case clearly demonstrated that lack of collaboration between school and home can prevent a child from getting necessary help to address his behavior problems. Teacher 3 avoided conflict with Selim's parents by not talking with them about Selim's behavior or learning problems. Teacher 3 expressed that she felt too stressed by classroom demands to invest the time needed to involve Selim's parents. On the other hand Selim's parents stated that they felt mistrustful of Teacher 3, felt they lack the knowledge to help educate Selim, and also overwhelmed by life stress that they have little energy to be involved in Selim's schooling.

Previous literature on the effectiveness of the FSS program pointed out the importance of getting educators and parents on the same side in helping vulnerable children experience school success (Goly, Stiller, & Walker, 1998; Walker et al., 1998). In fact, developing a collaborative home and school working relationship whose focus is on joint problem-solving and the development of school success has been shown as a key element of program success (Walker et al., 1998). Although extensive support was provided by the program coach to establish a collaborative home and school working relationship, both Selim's parents and teacher continued to blame each other for Selim's problems at school. Different perspectives were provided by the program coach to both parties to redirect the conversations to the immediate needs of Selim. However, because of the ongoing disputes, getting the parties to move the discussion to concrete steps to address Selim's behavior problems became a challenge.

In summary, lack of program fidelity, having an overwhelming classroom environment with a large number of students, difficulty to deal with challenging behaviors, and the lack of collaboration and communication between Selim's parents and teacher might had a negative impact on the effectiveness of the FSS program with Selim.

Effectiveness of the FSS Program on Class-Wide Student Behaviors and Teacher Behaviors

The effectiveness of the FSS program and its impact on class-wide student behaviors and teacher behaviors was evaluated by comparing pre and post test scores on the Teacher Ratings of Behavior.

Teachers' test scores on the Teacher Ratings of Behavior showed that all participant teachers reported positive changes on class-wide student behaviors.

Although some of the teachers' preintervention scores remained the same after the intervention, there were positive changes on most items. Specifically, Teacher 1 and 4's post intervention ratings revealed a positive change in almost all items. These positive changes are also consistent with previous studies which showed that the FSS program produced significant positive change in class-wide student behaviors (Diken & Rutherford, 2005; Perkins-Rowe 2001).

The impact of the FSS program on class-wide teacher behaviors was evaluated by comparing pre and post test scores on the Teacher Ratings of Behavior. Teachers' pre and post test scores on the teacher behaviors indicated that there were significant positive changes on all teachers' teacher behaviors. Specifically, before the intervention, all participant teachers reported difficulty in being able to find opportunities to focus on students' appropriate behaviors by praising children. The teachers also reported that they were experiencing significant problems in their classrooms through spending a lot of time focusing on the inappropriate behavior of just few children, feeling like spending more time correcting inappropriate behavior rather than teaching, and constantly having to reprimand children for inappropriate behavior.

Consistent with the above difficulties that the teachers experienced, research showed that teachers give three to fifteen times as much attention to student misbehavior (e.g., talking out, fidgeting, out of seat behavior) than to positive behavior in their classrooms (Brophy, 1996; Martens & Meller, 1990; Walker et al., 1995). Children who display problem behaviors were less likely to receive encouragement from teachers for appropriate behavior and more likely to be punished for misbehavior than well-behaved children. Furthermore, research also showed that poorly managed classrooms have higher levels of classroom aggression and rejection that, in turn, influence the continuing escalation of individual child behavior problems (Kellam, Ling, Merisca, Brown, & Ialongon, 1988). On the other hand, this study revealed that when the teachers used their attention selectively to reinforce positive behavior (while ignoring inappropriate behavior), they observed a dramatic impact on the behavior of targeted children as well as on the rest of the children in the classroom. Consistently, the teachers reported fewer problems with spending a lot of time focusing on the inappropriate behavior of just few children, constantly having to reprimand children for inappropriate behavior, feeling like they spend more time correcting inappropriate behavior rather than teaching.

These positive changes on the teacher behaviors and their impact on the targeted children were consistent with the results of previous research on the effectiveness of the FSS program Diken & Rutherford, 2005; Golly, et al., 2000; Overton, et al., 2002; Perkins-Rowe, 2001; Walker, et al., 1998). The findings from these studies showed that the FSS program was effective in developing more positive teaching approaches and effective classroom management skills of participant teachers while working with children with emotional and behavioral disorders.

The Perceptions of Participant Teachers and Parents Regarding the FSS Program

The perceptions of participant Turkish teachers and parents on the effectiveness of the FSS program and potential cultural barriers to the success of the program were explored using semi-structured interviews and the Social Validity survey.

The participant teachers' responses on the Social Validity survey revealed that all teachers, but Teacher 3, reported high levels of satisfaction with the FSS program. These findings were consistent with the previous study findings which showed that most participants generally indicated high levels of satisfaction with the program (Diken & Rutherford, 2005; Walker et al., 1998).

Despite the high level of satisfaction that the most teachers reported in this study, all teachers shared a common concern that they had difficulty finding the time needed for implementing the program. Teachers 1, 2, and 4 thought that the program was worth their time and effort. These teachers explained that the FSS program resulted in fewer AD/HD related

142

behaviors (e.g. excessive off-task behaviors, fidgeting, and disturbing other students), improved social skills, academic performance, and more parental involvement. The teachers also pointed out that the targeted children developed greater concentration, self confidence, improved self-expression, and more positive attitude toward school.

When asked about the use of the FSS program, all teachers agreed that implementing the FSS program with the use of red and green card was easy and effective. Teacher 4 pointed out that using a visual cue as a prompt and also as a reminder helped her target child to maximize his on-task behaviors. The teachers also agreed that the rewarding the target child when the target child reached his daily goals was very easy to do. In addition, Teacher 2 emphasized that rewarding the whole class fostered each of her students' care for the success of the target child and motivated meaningful group cooperation.

Although in general all teachers found the FSS program easy to use, they reported that they had difficulty finding the time to implement the program particularly when the implementation time span became longer. Participant teachers stated that they each had a very large class with 40 or 43 students and most students need individualized attention. Teacher 2 also explained that in general most children in the school district do not go kindergarten. Therefore, when children start first grade, they begin learning about how to stay seated and listen to someone for a long period of time. Teacher 2 pointed out that first grade is pretty challenging for a teacher since the teacher has to teach the children behavioral expectations along with reading and writing. She addressed that considering the challenges that a first grade teacher faces in Turkey, implementing an intervention program may put so much stress on the teacher. In addition, all participant teachers agreed that the time commitment required in the program may

143

ead Turkish teachers become skeptical to commit such a program.

These findings are similar with the previous study findings on the social validity of the program. Golly and colleagues' study revealed that the First Step to Success program was considered as somewhat costly and as appropriate only for children who have serious behavior problems (Golly, Stiller, & Walker, 1998). The researchers (1998) concluded that the severity of the child's behavior problems must be at some level corresponded to the effort involved in the implementation process. Another study also showed that the study participants indicated that the FSS program becomes more challenging as the target student progress through it. These results were normal because the FSS program is intended to be more demanding of the child in its later stages before it is ended after approximately 3 months (Walker et al., 1998). Golly and colleagues (1998) suggested that in such cases it is important to provide teachers with necessary psychological and empowering support as teachers deal with logistical barriers and problems.

When asked about what they liked most about the program, all teachers addressed that they liked the emphasis of positive attention to the target child's and other students' positive behaviors most. The teachers also reported that they began using the skills that they learned in dealing with the target children's antisocial behavior problems with their interactions with other students in the classroom. In addition, teachers stated that the FSS program fostered each of their student's care for the success of the target child and motivated meaningful group cooperation. In other words, teachers reported that their entire class became motivated to behave appropriately with the FSS program's focus on positive behavior.

Another important reason that the teachers liked the FSS program was the program's parent educational module. All participant teachers expressed a strong belief on the necessity of

144

active parent involvement in children's education. Teachers, 1, 3, and 4 further stressed that the lack of parental involvement was a serious contributor to the target children's school problems. Teachers 1, 2, and 4 expressed that as the program facilitated communication with parents, they were able to overcome many difficulties that they experienced with the parents before. The teachers stated that the parents of targeted children now have a clear understanding of what behaviors are expected to be considered appropriate or successful at school and how they can help their child by replacing the problem behavior with new skills to meet their needs.

Teacher 3 found that the FSS program was effective to some extent, but could not achieve its intended goals entirely because there was no collaboration between Selim's parents and herself. Teacher 3 expressed that she felt alone in teaching Selim to behave at school during the FSS implementation. She blamed Selim's parents for not providing appropriate care and supervision to Selim as they struggle with many issues including poverty, health problems, high family conflict, and social marginalization. Teacher 3 thought that her effect on Selim's behaviors was limited due to Selim's established behavioral problems at home such as hitting and lying. She suggested that Selim needed good parental modeling and a consistent behavior management not just at school but at home as well. Walker and colleagues (1998) demonstrated that the most frequently heard complaint by the teachers implementing the FSS program is that parental inconsistency and the lack of follow through form a program that limits the program's effectiveness. His study also pointed out that the First Step to Success Program does not appear to work well with the children who come from homes that are in chaos and need comprehensive supports and intervention just to live at a basic survival level.

All parents reported that their children were less hyperactive-inattentive and less angry as a result of the FSS program. In addition, parents also indicated that they became more satisfied with their parenting style and felt less confused and frustrated about how to help their children with their problem behaviors. More specifically, parents reported that they benefited greatly from learning about how to deal with difficult situations without getting angry, how to set limits, how to communicate with their children, and how to share school information with their children.

One of the purposes of this study was to identify potential cultural barriers to success of the FSS program. Semi-structured interviews with teachers and parents yielded various suggestions. Teachers 1 and 3 expressed that the lack of parental involvement in children's education influences their students' school achievements. Teachers pointed out most parents do not accept their role in motivating the children to understand the importance of academic achievement and to put effort to learn.

Teacher 4 also discussed that living with an extended family sometimes becomes a cultural barrier to success of such intervention programs. In her view, children of extended families usually do not have consistency and structure at home to learn necessary skills to do well socially and academically in Turkish culture. She believed that the differences in parenting styles of the grandparents and parents make children feel confused about behavioral expectations. Furthermore, Teacher 4 pointed out that most of her students who come from extended families are not encouraged to be self-sufficient and are not thought the skills of effort and responsibility since most grandparents are too helpful and overprotective over their grandchildren.

Parent 4 shared similar ideas with Teacher 4 and explained that her husband's mother and father lived with them. She had issues with disciplining her two children due to her different

146

parenting style than her father-in-law and mother-in-law. She stated that when she did not agree with her in laws on any subject, her husband's parents felt disrespected, which caused problems in her marriage.

When asked about potential cultural barriers to the success of the FSS program, Parent 1 explained that she thought that her son's teacher did not value her as a parent due to her low education level and the corresponding low income. She pointed out that when she joins parent teacher conferences she keeps quiet. Parents who have higher education level talk and she listens to them. Parent 1 addressed that no one ever asks for her ideas in such meetings. In her view, there is a clear discrimination, not just at her son's school but elsewhere in society. She thought that people who have more education and income are more valued than the people of low income and low education level.

Parent 3 shared similar ideas with Parent 1. She believed that her son's teacher did not value her family as they were an economically disadvantaged family and did not have higher education level. In addition, Parent 3 stated that her husband did not value education as much as she did. Since she only knew how to read and write, she did not feel capable of helping her son. Parent 3 pointed out that children who come from families with low education and low incomes should be provided with academic help services by schools.

The present study revealed that although most teachers want to be active partners in facilitating home-school involvement, many lack the confidence and training to work collaboratively with families. Realizing that student's cultural backgrounds, economic conditions, and home environments can profoundly affect their adjustment in school is critical for teachers. However, teachers also need to have the necessary skills to create a relationship

147

with parents that is mutually respectful and supportive. Such relationship should be non-blaming and nonhierarchical and should be based on a collaborative partnership. Collaboration refers to an assumption that families, children, and educators are doing the best they can; efforts are made to understand others' behavior and intentions rather than judge them as right or wrong. Accordingly, when schools and families make the effort to understand and educate each other, they often find more similarities than differences.

Indeed, Bronfenbrenner (1974) suggests that school recognition of the importance and benefits within culturally related variations in parental involvement will allow for stronger links between school and home. Accordingly, extant research on the parental involvement indicates that family involvement is one of the most promising ways to improve students' educational and social outcomes (Chavkin, 1993; Chavkin & Gonzalez, 1995; Henderson & Berla, 1994). However, parents of similar cultural and social values gain easier acceptance and access to the school environment, while families with diverse ethnic and SES backgrounds must adapt to the dominant school culture to become an advocate for their child. Delgado-Gaitan (1991) asserts that "ethnically diverse families living in poor socioeconomic conditions often face sustained isolation from the school culture, which can lead to miscommunication between parents and school" (p.21).

It is clear from the present study findings that teacher education programs should devote necessary attention to training teachers to gain necessary skills to build collaborative partnership with parents and to establish good communication about their students' school problems as well as their successes at school.

Implications for Practice

Overall, the participant children were displaying fewer problem behaviors of AD/HD and fewer social-emotional problematic behaviors according to both parents and teachers. These results provide further evidence meaningful changes in problem behaviors of children with ADHD as a result of the First Step to Success program.

The results of this study indicate compelling evidence that implementing a multicompenent early intervention program, the First Step to Success, can yield important benefits for children with AD/HD. As discussed above the program did not provide impressive results only with a child who was coming from a chaotic home environment, needed massive support, and more skilled teacher in the area of behavior management.

AD/HD is a disorder that affects a child's behavior and puts additional stress on the parent and overall family functioning. Accordingly, a recent review study revealed that the presence of AD/HD in children is linked to a) varying degrees with disturbances in family and marital disfunctioning, b) negative parents-child relationships), c) specific patterns of parental cognitions about child behavior and reduced parenting self-efficacy, and d) increased levels of parenting stress and parental psychopathology, especially when AD/HD is combined with conduct problems (Wash & Johnson, 2001).

The stressful, intense, and demanding nature of the child's AD/HD features are also likely to elevate negative reactions from other family members and to exert a disruptive effect on family relationships and on psychological functioning of parents (Wash & Johnson, 2001). In fact, research suggests that the family environment is negatively affected by the cumulative effects of child's AD/HD, as the child with AD/HD exhibits negative social behaviors which create a greater number of negative interactions between the parent and child.

The First Step to Success program has a strong parent training module in which parents are enlisted as partners with the school in teaching the target child skills at home that contribute to an enhanced school adjustment (communicating and sharing school, cooperation, setting limits, solving problems, making friends, and building confidence). However, when the program is used with children with AD/HD, it is necessary to adapt the program to address the unique needs of children with AD/HD. More specifically, families should be educated about the nature of the disorder, behavior management techniques, the effects of family dysfunction, conflict, and maladaptive processes on the child with AD/HD and empowered with knowledge and skills to contribute the child's social development. The use of their relationship as a positive corrective experience in changing the relationship patterns of the child requires insight and support over time. Family members should gain necessary skills to facilitate behavioral changes in their children and knowledge to recognize indicators of emerging negative manifestations that will require assessment and intervention modifications. Parents will need to learn the necessary skills not only to manage the chronic nature of the disorder but also the stress that they experience. Furthermore, parents who are educated in the description, causes, prognosis, and treatment of AD/HD are better able to foment behavioral change in their children (DuPaul, Guevremont, & Barkley, 1991).

Additionally, not only providing parents with necessary knowledge but also determining behavioral expectations for home and incorporating clearly defined behavioral expectations to HomeBase component of the FSS program not only increases the continuity of the program but also, the intensity. Indeed, parents are generally with their children more than are teachers; this

150

puts parents in the top position to create difficult behavior environments, or, more constructively, to provide long-term interventions.

Parents are essential parts of the multi-component interventions. Indeed, in conducting any intervention, there must be a continuity of behavioral expectations between home and school. Discussing behavioral strategies, rewards, and limits with parents to ensure continuity of an approach to dealing with challenging behaviors between home and school is crucial. In that way, parents can encourage the targeted skills and performance at home and in different peer groups.

In addition, incorporating a teacher training module on the nature of the disorder and behavioral and instructional methods to address the specific needs of children with ADHD would be an important adaptation for the First Step to Success program to achieve the expected behavioral changes while working with children with AD/HD. Indeed, research showed that teachers with more training and experience in the area of AD/HD expressed more confidence in modifying the behavior of children with the disorder (Reid, Vasa, Maag, & Wright, 1994).

Finally, this study suggests that when the First Step to Success program is implemented under challenging conditions, investigating ways of helping teachers while the teachers implementing the program and teaching other students at the same time is extremely important. Most teachers working in developing countries like Turkey face common issues such as large classes, lack of teaching supplies and equipment, and lack of resources on behavioral and instructional methods to teach diverse needs students.

One way to help teachers might be providing teachers with a classroom aide. Helping teachers with their teaching responsibilities may diminish the stress that they feel during the implementation of the program and in turn increase the program fidelity.

Without intervention children with AD/HD will likely remain frustrated, angry, stressed, unmotivated, and unsuccessful in school and they will carry these problems to their future. Therefore, helping children with AD/HD with well-designed interventions is crucially important. The First Step to Success program is a successful early intervention program which involves careful and sensitive consideration of the individual characteristics of children, the intensity of behaviors, specific strengths and weaknesses, social and emotional needs, environmental and family factors. However, incorporating an AD/HD training module designed specifically for teachers and parents would strengthen the program outcomes and in turn, increase the effectives of the program with children with AD/HD.

Limitations

This study has provided encouraging evidence of the effectiveness of the FSS program with Turkish children with AD/HD. As with any study, however, it is important to recognize its inherent limitations.

The first limitation of the study is that the small sample size limits the generalization of conclusions; however, the findings from this study support further study of the benefits of the FSS program for children with AD/HD, using a larger sample size. This study involved three groups of participants (4 participants in each group): 4 participant Turkish children (4 first-graders), 4 Turkish teachers, and 4 Turkish parents. Given that the intervention package was initiated with only 4 children, generalization to other children with AD/HD needs replication.

The second limitation is that the treatment fidelity of the program was provided by the FSS program for only the CLASS component. However, as the program has two components, the CLASS and HomeBase, providing parents with a monitoring form might strengthen the program fidelity. In addition, direct observations of the program's implementation in the classroom would provide conclusive evidence on the effectiveness of the FSS program on targeted children's problem behaviors.

The last limitation of this study is that the observational data were gathered in the classroom context which was considered to include high frequency of academic engagement behaviors. Although, before collecting observational data for the research, the researcher informed the class that she would observe their teacher, and positioned herself in a least distractive place in the classroom for the target children, the target children might have been influenced by having an observer in their classroom. The target children may have displayed more on-task behaviors than usual during the observations.

Implications for Research

Despite the limitations, this study is an important study that makes significant contribution to establishing an effective intervention option for children with AD/HD. Subsequent studies are needed to build on this impressive piece of work, particularly as it relates to the children with AD/HD.

First, a closer look at characteristics of children with AD/HD, especially effects of the First Step to Success program on social skills of children with AD/HD need further clarification. Using an instrument specifically designed to measure children's social skills would strengthen the conclusions that could be drawn from any study exploring the effectiveness of the FSS program.

Second, the effectiveness of the FSS program on problem behaviors of children with AD/HD should be examined with a larger sample from various cultural groups. A larger sample size may give more information related to variables that lead success or failure of the FSS program. In fact, factors or dynamics involved in a child's home environment (e.g., high parental conflict, poverty, physical abuse) and school and classroom environment (e.g., large class size, teacher's lack of classroom management skills, teacher's stress level) that can interfere with the success of the First Step to Success program should be identified and effects of such factors should be explored in future studies.

Third, the range of behaviors that had been observed in this study should be extended to various types of behaviors (e.g., play behaviors) and should be observed in different settings (e.g., classroom, playground) in different time periods by using various data collection techniques. In addition semi-structured interviews might be conducted with participant children before and after the intervention in order to get an insight on how such interventions affect children's emotions and behaviors.

REFERENCES

Achenbach, T. M. (1978). The child behavior profile: I. Boys aged 6-11. *Journal of consulting and Clinical Psychology, 46*, 478-488.

Achenbach, T. M. (1991a). *Manual for the Child Behavior Checklist/4-18 and 1991 profile.* Burlington, VT: University of Vermont, Department of Psychiatry.

Achenbach, T. M. (1991b). *Manual for the Teacher's Report Form and 1991 profile.* Burlington, VT: University of Vermont, Department of Psychiatry.

Achenbach, T. M. (1996). Subtyping ADHD: The request for suggestions about relating empirically based assessment to DSM-IV. *The ADHD Report, 4*, 5-9.

Achenbach, T. M., & Edelbrock, C. S. (1978). The classification of child psychopathology: A review and analysis of empirical efforts. *Psychological Bulletin, 85*, 1275–1301.

Achenbach, T. M., & Edelbrock, C. S. (1983). *Manual for the Child Behavior Checklist and revised child behavior profile.* Burlington, VT: University of Vermont, Department of Psychiatry.

American Psychiatric Association. (1994). *Diagnostic and statistical manual of mental disorders* (4th ed.). Washington, DC: Author.

Anastopoulos, A. D., Barkley, R. A., & Shelton, T. L. (1996). Family-based treatment: Psychosocial intervention for children and adolescents with ADHD. In E. D. Hibbs & P. S. Jensen (Eds.), *Psychosocial treatments for child and adolescent disorders: Empirically based strategies for clinical practice* (pp. 267-284). Washington. D.C. American Psychological Association.

Anastopoulos, A. D., Guevremont, D. C., Shelton, T. L., & DuPaul, G. J. (1992). Parenting stress among families of children with attention deficit hyperactivity disorder. *Journal of Abnormal Child Psychology, 20*(5), 503-520.

Ang, R. P., & Hughes, J. N. (2002). Differential benefits of skills training with antisocial youth based on group composition: A meta-analytic investigation. *The School Psychology Review, 31*(2), 164- 185.

Arnold, L. E., Abikoff, H. B., Cantwell, D. P., Connors, C. K., Elliott, G., Greenhill, L. L., et al. (1997). National Institute of Mental Health collaborative multimodal treatment study of children with ADHD (the MTA). Archives *of General Psychiatry, 54,* 865–870.

Angold, A., Costello, E. J., & Erkanli, A. (1999). Comorbidity. *The Journal of Child Psychology and Psychiatry and Allied Disciplines, 40*(1), 57-87.

Atkins, M. S., & Stoff, D. M. (1993). Instrumental and hostile aggression in childhood disruptive behavior disorders. *Journal of Abnormal Child Psychology, 21,* 165-178.

Aydogdu, A. (2001). Dikkat eksikligi hiperaktivite bozuklugu ve yaygin gelisimsel bozukluk tanisi alan cocuklarin annelerinin bakim gereksinimleri ve cocuklarini algilama duzeyleri. (Perceptions of the mothers of children with pervasive developmental disorders and attention deficit hyperactivity disorder on their children and their care needs). Unpublished master's thesis, Istanbul University, Istanbul, Turkey.

Barkley, R. A. (1990). *Attention-deficit hyperactivity disorder: A handbook for diagnosis and treatment.* New York: Guilford Press.

Barkley, R.A. (1997a). *ADHD and the nature of self-control.* New York: Guilford Press.

Barkley, R.A. (1997b). *Defiant children: A clinician's manual for assessment and parent training* (2nd ed.), New York: Guilford Press.

Barkley, R.A. (1997c). ADHD and the nature of self-control. New York: Guilford Press.

Barkley, R. A. (1998). *Attention-deficit hyperactivity disorder: A handbook for diagnosis and treatment* (2nd ed.). New York: Guilford Press.

Barkley, R. A. (2000). *Taking Charge of ADHD*. New York: The Guilford Press.

Barkley, R. A., Fischer, M., Edelbrock, C. S. & Smallish, L. (1990). The adolescent outcome of hyperactive children diagnosed by research criteria: I. An 8 year prospective follow-up study. Journal of American Academy of Child and Adolescent Psychiatry, 29, 546-557.

Berkowitz, L. (1989). Frustration-aggression hypothesis: Examination and reformulation. *Psychological Bulletin, 106(1),* 59-73.

Berry, C., Shaywitz, S., & Shaywitz, B. (1985). Girls with attention deficit disorder: A silent minority? A report on behavioral and cognitive characteristics. *Pediatrics, 76,* 801-809.

Biederman, J., Faraone, S. V., Millberger, S., Curtis, S., Chen, L., Marrs, A., et al. (1996). Predictors of persistence and remission of ADHD into adolescence: Results from a four-year prospective follow-up study. *Journal of the American Academy of Child and Adolescent, 35,* 343–351.

Bierman, K. L., Miller, C. L., & Stabb, S. D. (1987). Improving the social behavior and peer acceptance of rejected boys: Effects of social skills training with instructions and prohibitions. *Journal of Consulting and Clinical Psychology, 55,* 194–200.

Blachman, D. R., & Hinshaw, S. (2002). Patterns of friendship among girls with and without attention-deficit/hyperactivity disorder. *Journal of Abnormal Child Psychology, 30,* 625-640.

Bloomquist, M. L., Michael, L., August, G. J., Cohen, C., & Doyle, A. (1997). Social problem

    solving in hyperactive-aggressive children: How and what they think in conditions of

    automatic and controlled processing. *Journal of Clinical and Child Psychology, 26,* 172-

    180.

Braaten, E. B., & Rosén, L.A. (2000). Self-regulation of affect in attention deficit-hyperactivity

    disorder (ADHD) and non-ADHD boys: Differences in empathic responding. *Journal of*

    Consulting and Clinical Psychology, 68, 313-321.

Brown, R., Madan-Swain, A., & Baldwin, K. (1991). Gender differences in a clinic-referred

    sample of attention-deficit disordered children. *Child Psychiatry and Human*

    Development, 22, 111-128.

Bronfenbrenner, U. (1974). Is early intervention effective? *Teachers College Record, 76,* 279-

    303.

Byrne, J. M., DeWolfe, N. A., & Bawden, H. N. (1998). Assessment of attention-deficit

    hyperactivity disorder in preschoolers. *Child Neuropsychology, 4,* 49-66.

Campbell, S. B., & Ewing, L. J. (1990). Follow-up of hard to manage preschoolers: adjustment

    at age 9 and predictors of continuing symptoms. *Journal of Child Psychology and*

    Psychiatry, 31, 871-889.

Carlson, C. L., & Bunner, M. R. (1993). Effects of methylphenidate on the academic

    performance of children with attention-deficit hyperactivity disorder and learning

    disabilities. *School Psychology Review, 22,* 184-198.

Casey, R. J. (1996). Emotional competence in children with externalizing and internalizing

    disorders. In M. Lewis & M. W. Sullivan (Eds.), *Emotional development in atypical*

158

children (pp. 161–183). Mahwah, NJ: Erlbaum.

Charles, L., & Schain, R. (1981). A four-year follow-up study of the effects of methylphenidate on the behavior and academic achievement of hyperactive children. *Journal of Abnormal Child Psychology, 9*, 495-505.

Chavkin, N.F. (Ed.). (1993). *Families and schools in a pluralistic society.* Albany: State University of New York Press.

Cicchetti, D., Ackerman, B. R., & Izard, C. E. (1995). Emotions and emotion regulation in developmental psychopathology. *Development and Psychopathology, 7*, 1-10.

Cole, P. M., Zahn-Waxler, C. & Smith, D.K. 91994). Expressive control during a disappointment: Variations related to preschoolers' behavior problems. *Developmental Psychology, 30(6)*, 835-846.

Crick, N. R. & Dodge, K. A. (1994). A review and reformulation of social information processing mechanism in children's social adjustment. *Psychological Bulletin, 115*, 74-101.

Crick, N. R. & Dodge, K. A. (1996). Social information processing mechanisms in reactive and proactive aggression. *Child Development, 67*, 993-10002.

Delgado-Gaitan, C. (1991). Involving parents in school: A process of empowerment. *American Journal of Education, 100*, 20-46.

Diener, M. B., & Milich, R. (1997). The effects of positive feedback on social interactions in children with ADHD: A test of the self-protective hypothesis. *Journal of Clinical Child Psychology, 26*, 256-263.

Diken, I. (2004). *First Step to Success early Intervention Program: A study of effectiveness with children in and American Indian community school.* Unpublished doctoral dissertation, Arizona State University, Phoenix.

Diken, I. H., & Rutherford, R. B. (2005). First Step to Success early intervention program: A study of Effectiveness with Native-American children. *Education and Treatment of Children, 28,* 445-465.

Dodge, K. (1993). The future of research on conduct disorder. *Development and Psychopathology, 5,* 311-320.

Dodge, K. A., & Coie, J. D. (1987). Social-information-processing factors in reactive and proactive aggression in children's peer groups. *Journal of Personality and Social Psychology, 53(6),* 1146-1158.

Dodge, K. A., & Feldman, E. (1990). Issues in social cognition and sociometric status. In S. R. Asher & J. D. Coie (Eds.), *Peer rejection in childhood* (pp.119-155). New York: Cambridge University Press.

Dodge, K. A., Pettit, G. S. (2003). A biopsychosocial model of the development of chronic conduct problems in adolescence. *Developmental Psychology, 39(2),* 349-371.

Dodge, K. A., & Somberg, D. R. (1987). Hostile attributional biases among aggressive boys are exacerbated under conditions of threats to the self. *Child Development, 58,* 213-234.

Dodge, K. A., & Tomlin, A. M. (1987). Utilization of self-schemas as mechanism of interpretational bias in aggressive children. *Social Cognition, 5,* 280-300.

Dodge, K. A., Lochman, J. E., Harnish, J. D., Bates, J. E., & Pettit, G. S. (1997). Reactive and proactive aggression in school children and psychiatrically impaired chronically assaultive youth. *Journal of Abnormal Psychology, 106*, 37-51.

DuPaul, G. J., Guevremont, D. C., & Barkley, R. A. (1992). Behavioral treatment of attention-deficit hyperactivity disorder in the classroom: The use of the attention training system. *Behavior Modification, 16*(2), 204- 225.

DuPaul, G. J., & Eckert, T. L. (1994). The effects of social skills curricula: Now you see them, now you don't. *School Psychology Quarterly, 9*(2), 113-132.

DuPaul, G. J., McGoey, K. E., Eckert, T. L., & VanBrakle, J. (2001). Social skills problems of children with ADHD. *Journal of American Child Adolescent Psychiatry, 40*, 508-515.

DuPaul, G. J., Power, T. J., Anastopoulos, A. D., Reid, R. (1998). *ADHD Rating Scale IV Manual*. New York: Guilford Press.

DuPaul, G. J., & Stoner, G. (2003). *ADHD in the schools: Assessment and intervention strategies* (2nd ed.). New York: Guilford Press.

Ebert, D., Martus, P. (1994). Somatization as a core symptom of melancholic type Depression: Evidence from a cross-cultural study. *Journal of Affect Disorder, 32*, 253-256.

Edelbrock, C., & Achenbach, T. (1984). The teacher version of the Child Behavior Profile: I. Boys age 6-11. *Journal of Consulting and Clinical Psychology, 52*, 207-217.

Edelbrock, C., & Costello, A. J. (1988). Convergence between statistically derived behavior problem syndromes and child psychiatric diagnoses. *Journal of Abnormal Child Psychology, 16*, 219–231.

Eisenberg, N. (2001). The core and correlates of affective social competence. *Social Development, 10*, 120-124.

Eisenberg, N., Cumberland, A., Spinrad, T. L., Fabes, R. A., Shepard, S., Reiser, M., Murphy, B.
C., Losoya, S. H., & Guthrie, I. K. (2001). The relations of regulation and emotionality to
children's externalizing and internalizing problem behavior. *Child Development, 72,*
1112-1134.

Eisenberg, N., Fabes, R. A., Murphy, B., Maszk, P., Smith, M., & Karbon, M. (1995). The role
of emotionality and regulation in children's social functioning: A longitudinal study.
Child Development, 66, 1360-1384.

Eisenberg, N., Fabes, R. A., Nyman, M., Bernzweig, J., & Pinuelas, A. (1994). The relations of
emotionality and regulation to children's anger-related reactions. *Child Development, 65,*
109-128.

Eisenberg, N., Fabes, R. A. Shepard, S., Murphy, B. C., Guthrie, I. K., Jones, S., Friedman, J.,
Pouline, R., & Maszk, B. C., (1997). Contemporaneous and longitudinal prediction of
children's social functioning from regulation and emotionality. *Child Development, 68,*
642-664.

Eisenberg, N., Guthrie, I. K., Fabes, R. A., Shepard, S. Losoya, S., Murphy, B. C., Jones, Poulin,
R., and Reiser, M. (2000). Prediction of elementary school children's externalizing
problem behaviors from attentional and behavioral regulation and negative emotionality.
Child Development, 71(5), 1367-1382.

Erhardt, D., & Hinshaw, S. (1994). Initial sociometric impressions of attention-deficit
hyperactivity disorder and comparison boys: Predictions from social behaviors and from
nonbehavioral variables. *Journal of Consulting and Clinical Psychology, 62,* 833-842.

Erman, O. (2001). Parent and teacher training in attention deficit hyperactivity disorder: Review.

Cocuk ve Genclik Ruh Sagligi Dergisi, 8, 39-47.

Erol, N., Arslan, L. B., & Akcakin, M. (1995). The adaptation and standardiazion of the Child

    Bbehvaior Checklist among 6-18-year-old Turkish cildren. In J. A. Sergeant (Ed.).

    Eunenthydis; European approaches to hyperkinetic disorder (pp. 97-113). Zurich,

    Switzerland: Fotorotar.

Ersan, E. E., Dogan, O., Dogan, S., Sumer, H. (2004). The distribution of symptoms of attention

    deficit/hyperactivity disorder and oppositional defiant disorder in school age children in

    Turkey. *European and Child Adolescent Psychiatry, 13*, 354-361.

Faraone, S. V., & Biederman, J. (1998). Neurobiology of attention-deficit hyperactivity disorder.

    Biological Psychiatry, 44, 951–958.

Fletcher, K.E., Fisher, M., Barkley, R. A., & Smallish, L. (1996). A sequential analysis of the

    mother-adolescent interactions of ADHD, ADHD/ODD, and normal teenagers during

    neutral and conflict discussions. *Journal of Abnormal Child Psychology, 24,* 271-297.

Flicek, M. (1992). Social status of boys with both academic problems and attention deficit

    hyperactivity disorder. *Journal of Abnormal Child Psychology, 20,* 353-365.

Gaub, M. M., & Carlson, C. L. (1997a). Behavioral characteristics of DSM-IV subtypes in a

    school based population. *Journal of Abnormal Child Psychology, 25,* 103-111.

Gaub, M., & Carlson, C. (1997b). Gender differences in ADHD: A meta-analysis and critical

    review. *Journal of the American Academy of Child Adolescent Psychiatry, 36,* 1036-

    1045.

Golly, A., Sprague, J., & Walker, H. M. (2000). The First Step to Success program: An analysis

    of outcomes with identical twins across multiple baselines. *Behavioral Disorders, 25,*

170-182.

Golly, A., Sprague, J., Walker, H. M., Beard, K., & Gorham, G. (2000). The First Step to

Success program: An analysis of outcomes with identical twins across multiple baselines.

Behavioral Disorders, 25, 170-182.

Golly, A. M., Stiller, B., & Walker, H. M. (1998). First Step to Success: Replication and social

validation of an early intervention program. *Journal of Emotional and Behavioral*

Disorders, 6, 243-250.

Goldstein, S., & Goldstein, M. (1998). *Managing attention deficit hyperactivity disorder in*

children (2nd ed.), New York: John Wiley & Sons, Inc.

Guevremont, D. C., & Dumas, M. C. (1994). Peer relationship problems and disruptive behavior

disorders. *Journal of Emotional and Behavioral Disorders, 2*, 164-173.

Greenwood, P. W. (1995). *The cost effectiveness of early intervention as a strategy for reducing*

violent crime. Paper prepared for the University of California Policy Seminar Crime

Project, RAND, Santa Monica, CA.

Gresham, F. M., MacMillan, D. L., Bocian, K. M., Ward, S. L., & Forness, S. R. (1998).

Comorbidity of hyperactivity-impulsivity-inattention and conduct problems: Risk factors

in social, affective, and academic domains. *Journal of Abnormal Child Psychology, 26*,

393-406.

Hartup, W. (1983). Peer relations. In E. M. Hetherington (Vol. Ed.) & P. H. Mussen (Series Ed.),

Handbook of child psychology: Vol. 4. *Socialization, personality, and social*

development (pp. 103-196). New York: Wiley.

Henderson, A.T. & Berla, N. (Eds.) (1994). *A new generation of evidence: The family is critical to student achievement.* Washington, DC: National Committee for Citizens in Education.

Hinshaw, S. P. (1987). On the distinction between attentional deficits/hyperactivity and conduct problems/aggression in child psychopathology. *Psychological Bulletin, 101,* 443-463.

Hinshaw, S. P. (1992). Externalizing behavior problems and academic underachievement in childhood and adolescence: Causal relationships and underlying mechanisms. *Psychological Bulletin, 111,* 127–155.

Hinshaw, S. P. (1994). *Attention deficits and hyperactivity in children.* California, CA, Sage.

Hinshaw, S. P., Henker, B., Whalen, C. K., Erhardt, D., & Dunnington, R. E. (1989). Aggressive, prosocial, and nonsocial behavior in hyperactive boys: Dose effects of methylphenidate in naturalistic settings. *Journal of Consulting and Clinical Psychology, 57,* 636-643.

Hinshaw, S. P., Lahey, B. B., & Hart, E. L. (1993). Issues of taxonomy and comorbidity in the development of conduct disorder. *Development and Psychopathology, 5,* 31-49.

Hinshaw, S. P., & Melnick, S. (1995). Peer relations in boys with attention deficit hyperactivity disorder with and without comorbid aggression. *Development and Psychopatology, 7,* 627-647.

Hodgens, J. B., Cole, J., & Boldizar, J. (2000). Peer-based differences among boys with ADHD. *Journal of Clinical Child Psychology, 29,* 443-452.

Hops, H., & Walker, H. M. (1988). CLASS: Contingencies for learning academic and social skills. Seattle, WA: Educational Achievement Systems.

Hoza, B., Pelham, W. E., Dobbs, J., Owens, J. S., & Pillow, D. R. (2002). Do boys with attention-deficit/hyperactivity disorder have positive illusory self-concepts? *Journal of Abnormal Psychology, 111,* 268-278.

Hoza, B., Pelham, W., Milich, R. R., & McBride, K. (1993). The self-perception and attributions of the attention deficit hyperactivity disordered and nonreferred boys. *Journal of Abnormal Child Psychology, 21,* 271-286.

Hubbard, J. A., Dodge, K. A., Cillessen, A. H. N., Coie, J. D., & Scwartz, D. (2001). The dyadic nature of Social Information Processing in boys' reactive and proactive aggression. *Journal of Personality and Social Psychology, 80(2),* 268-280.

Johnston, C., Pelham, W. E., & Murphy, H. A. (1985). Peer relationships in ADHD and normal children: A developmental analysis of peer and teacher ratings. *Journal of Abnormal Child Psychology, 13,* 89-100.

Johnston, C., & Mash, E. J. (2001) Families of children with attention-deficit/hyperactivity disorder: Review and recommendations for future research. *Clinical and Family Psychology Review, 4,* 183-207.

Joseph, G. E., & Strain, P. S. (2003). Comprehensive evidence based social emotional curricula for young children: An analysis of efficacious adoption potential. *Topics in Early Childhood Special Education, 23,* 65-76.

Kashani, J. H., Jones, M. R., Bumby, K. M., & Thomas, L. A. (1999). Youth violence: Psychosocial risk factors, treatment, prevention, and recommendations. *Journal of Emotional and Behavioral Disorders, 7,* 200-210.

Kazdin, A. E. (1987). Treatment of antisocial behavior in children: Current status and future directions. *Psychological Bulletin, 102(2),* 187-203.

Keenyan, K., Shaw, D.S., Walsh, B., Delliquadri, E., & Giovannelli, J. (1997). DSM-III-R disorders in preschool children from low-income families. *Journal of the American Academy of Child and Adolescent Psychiatry, 36,* 620–627.

Kellam, S. G., Ling, X., Merisca, R., Brown, C. H., & Ialongon, N. (1988). The effect of the level of aggression in the first grade classroom on the course and malleability of aggressive behavior into middle school. *Development and Psychopathology, 10,* 165-185.

Kerr. M. M., & Nelson, C. M. (1989). *Strategies for managing behavior problems in the classroom.* Columbus: Chaiks E. Merrill.

Klein, R. G., & Mannuzza, S. (1991). Long-term outcome of hyperactive children: A review. *Journal of the American Academy of Child and Adolescent Psychiatry, 30,* 383-387.

Lahey, B. B., Bischaughency, E. A., & Hynd, G. W., Carlson, C. L., & Nieves, N. (1987). Attention deficit disorder with and without hyperactivity: Comparison of behavioral characteristics of clinic referred children. *Journal of American-Academy of Child and Adolescent Psychiatry, 26,* 718-723.

Lahey, B. B., Schaughency, E. A., Strauss, C. C., & Frame, C. L. (1984). Are attention deficit disorders with and without hyperactivity similar or dissimilar disorders? *Journal of the American Academy of Child Psychiatry, 23,* 302-309.

Lahey, B. B., Schaughency, E., Hynd, G., Carlson, C., & Nieves, N. (1987). Attention deficit disorder with and without hyperactivity: Comparison of behavioral characteristics of clinic-referred children. *Journal of the American Academy of Child Psychiatry, 26,* 718-723.

Landau, S., & Milich, R. (1990). Assessment of children's social status and peer relations. In A. M. La Greca (Ed.), *Through the eyes of child: Obtaining self-reports from children and adolescents* (pp. 259-291). Boston: Allyn and Bacon.

Landau, S., & Milich, R. (1998). Social communication patterns of attention-deficit-disordered boys. *Journal of Abnormal Psychology, 16,* 69-81.

Landau, S., Milich. R., & Diener, M. B. (1998). Peer relations of children with attention deficit hyperactivity disorder. *Reading & Writing Quarterly: Overcoming Learning Difficulties, 14,* 83-105.

Landau, S., & Moore, L. A. (1991). Social skills deficits in children with attention-deficit hyperactivity disorder. *School Psychology Review, 20,* 235-251.

Lavigne, J.V., Gibbons, R.D., Christoffel, K.K., Arend, R., Rosenbaum, D., & Binns, H., et al. (1996). Prevalence rates and correlates of psychiatric disorders among preschool children. *Journal of the American Academy of Child and Adolescent Psychiatry, 35,* 204–214.

Leff, S. S., Power, T. J., Manz, P. H., Costigan, T. E., & Nabors, L A. (2001). School-based aggression prevention programs for young children: Current status and implications for violence prevention. *School Psychology Review, 30,* 344-362.

Lemery, K., Essex, M.J., & Smider, N.A. (2002). Revealing the relation between temperament and behavior problem symptoms by eliminating measurement confounding: Expert ratings and factor analyses. *Child Development, 73,* 867-882.

Lien, T. S., & Kamps, D. (2005). Replication study of the First Step to Success early intervention program. *Behavioral Disorders, 31,* 18-32.

Lochman, J. E., & Dodge, K. A. (1994). Social-cognitive processes of severely violent, moderately aggressive, and nonaggressive boys. *Journal of Consulting and Clinical*

168

Psychology, 62, 366-374.

Lewis, T. J., Sugai, G., & Colvin, G. (1998). Reducing problem behavior through a school-wide system of effective behavioral support: Investigation of a school-wide social skills training program and contextual interventions. *School Psychology Review, 27*, 446-459.

Maedgen, J. W., & Carlson, C. L., (2000). Social Functioning and emotional regulation in the attention deficit hyperactivity disorder subtypes. *Journal of Clinical Child Psychology, 29*, 30-42.

Mannuzza, S., Klein, R. G., Bonagura, N., Konig, P. H., & Shenker, R. (1988). Hyperactive boys almost grown up: II. Status of subjects without a mental disorder. *Archives of General Psychiatry, 45,* 13-18.

Martens, B. K., & Meller, P. J. (1989). Influence of child and classroom characteristics on acceptability of interventions. *Journal of School Psychology, 27*, 237-245.

McGoey, K. E., Eckert, T. L., & DuPaul, G. J. (2002). Early intervention for preschool-age children with ADHD: A literature review. *Journal of Emotional and Behavioral Disorders, 10*, 14-28.

Melnick, S. M., & Hinshaw, S. P. (1996). What they want and what they get: The social goals of boys with ADHD and comparison boys. *Journal of Abnormal Child Psychology, 24,* 169–185.

Melnick, S. M., & Hinshaw, S. P. (2000). Emotion regulation and parenting in AD/HD and comparison boys: Linkages with social behaviors and preference. *Journal of Abnormal Child Psychology, 28,* 73-86.

Mercugliano, M., Power, T. J., & Blum, N. J. (1990). The clinician's practical guide to attention-deficit/hyperactivity disorder. Baltimore, MD: Paul H. Brookes Publishing.

Milich, R. (1994). The response of children with ADHD to failure: If at first you don't succeed, do you try, try again? *School Psychology Review, 23,* 11-18.

Milich, R., & Dodge, K, A. (1984). Social information processing in child psychiatric populations. *Journal of Abnormal child Psychology, 12,* 471-490.

Miller, P. A. & Eisenberg, N. (1998). The relation of empathy to aggressive and externalizing/antisocial behavior. *Psychological Bulletin, 103,* 324-344.

Mikami, A. Y., & Hinshaw, S. P. (2003). Buffers of peer rejection among girls with and without ADHD: The role of popularity with adults and goal-directed solitary play. *Journal of Abnormal Child Psychology, 31,* 381-397.

Mott, P., & Krane, A. (1994). Interpersonal cognitive problem-solving and childhood social competence. *Cognitive Therapy and Research, 18,* 127-141.

Mrug, S., Hoza, B., & Gerdes, A. C. (2001). Children with attention-deficit/hyperactivity disorder: Peer relationships and peer-oriented interventions. In C. A. Erdley & D. W. Nangle (Ed.), *The role of friendship in psychological adjustment* (pp.51-77). San Francisco, CA: Jossey-Bass.

Noam, G., & Hermann, C. A. (2002). Where education and mental health meet: developmental prevention and early intervention in schools. *Development and Psychopathology, 14,* 861-875.

Oncu, B., Oner, O., Oner, P., Erol, N. Aysev, A., & Canat, S. (2004). Symptoms defined by parents and teachers' ratings in attention deficit hyperactivity disorder: Changes with age. *Canadian Journal of Psychiatry, 49,* 487-491.

Overton, S., McKenzie, L., King, K., & Osborne, J. (2002). Replication of the First Step to

    Success Model: A multiple-case study of implementation effectiveness. *Behavioral*

    Disorders, 28, 1, 40-56.

Ozdemir, S. (2006*)*. Burnout among Turkish Teachers of Students with Attention Deficit

    Hyperactivity Disorder, *Education and Treatment of Children, 29* (4), 693-709.

Ozcan, C. T. (2002). Dikkat eksikligi ve hiperaktivite bozuklugu olan cocuklarin anne-

    babalarinin empati duzeyi ve aile islevlerinin incelenmesi. (The emphatic skills and

    family functioning of parents of the children with attention deficit hyperactivity disorder).

    Unpublished master's thesis, GATA, Saglik Bilimleri Enstitusu, Hemsirelik Yuksek

    Okulu, Ankara, Turkey.

Parker, J.G., & Asher, S. R. (1987). Peer relations and later personal adjustment: Are low-

    accepted children at risk? *Psychological Bulletin, 102,* 357-389.

Paternite, C. E., Loney, J., Salisbury, H., & Whaley, M. A. (1999). Childhood inattention-

    overactivity, aggression, and stimulant medication history as predictors of young adult

    outcomes. *Journal of Child and Adolescent Psychopharmacology, 9,* 169-184.

Pelham, W. E., & Bender, M. E. (1982). Peer relationships in hyperactive children: Description

    and treatment. *Advances in Learning and Behavioral Disabilities, 1,* 365-436.

Perkins-Rowe, K. A. (2001). Direct and collateral effects of the First Step to Success program:

    Replication and extension of findings. In I. Diken, (2004). *First Step to Success early*

    Intervention Program: A study of effectiveness with children in and American Indian

    community school. Unpublished doctoral dissertation, Arizona State University, Phoenix.

Power, T. J., Doherty, B. J., Panichelli-Mindel, S. M., Karustis, J. L., Eiraldi, R. B.,

Anastopoulos, A. D., et al. (1998). The predictive validity of parent and teacher reports of ADHD symptoms. *Journal of Psychopathology and Behavioral Assessment, 20,* 57-81.

Reid, J. (1993). Prevention of conduct disorder before and after school entry: Relating interventions to developmental findings. *Development and Psychopathology, 5,* 243-262.

Reid, R., Maag, J. W., Vasa, S. F., & Wright, G. (1994). Who are the children with attention-deficit hyperactivity disorder? A school-based survey. *Journal of Special Education, 28,* 117-137.

Sandstrom, M. J., & Cramer, P. (2003). Girl's use of defense mechanisms following peer rejection. *Journal of Personality, 71(4),* 605-627.

Shekim, W. O., Cantwell, D. P., Kashani, J., Beck, N., Martin, J., & Rosenberg, J. (1986). Dimensional and categorical approaches to the diagnosis of attention deficit disorder in children. *Journal of the American Academy of Child Psychiatry, 25,* 653-658.

Shelton, T. L., Barkley, r. A., Crosswait, C., Moorehouse, M., Fletcher, K., Barrett, S., et al. (2000). Multimethod psychoeducational intervention for preschool children with disruptive behavior: Two-year post-treatment follow-up. *Journal of Abnormal Child Psychology, 28,* 253-266.

Sheridan, S. M. (1998). Social skills training for ADHD children S. Goldstein, & M. Goldstein, (Eds.), *Managing attention deficit hyperactivity disorder in children* (pp. 592-612). New York: John Wiley & Sons, Inc.

Smith, A. M., & O'Leary, S. G. (1995). Attributions and arousal as predictors of maternal discipline. *Cognitive Therapy Research, 19,* 459-471.

Southam-Gerow, M. A. & Kendall, P. C. (2002). Emotion regulation and understanding:

Implications for child psychopathology and therapy. *Clinical Psychology Review, 22,* 189-222.

Stormont-Spurgin, M., & Zentall, S. S. (1995). Contributing factors in the manifestation of aggression in preschoolers with hyperactivity. *Journal of Child Psychology and Psychiatry, 36,* 491–509.

Stormont, M. (2001). Social outcomes of children with AD/HD: Contributing factors and implications for practice. *Psychology in the Schools, 38*(6), 521-531.

Taylor, J. F. (1994). *Helping your hyperactive/attention deficit child.* CA: Prima.

Taylor, E. (1999). Developmental neuropsychopathology of attention deficit and impulsiveness. *Development and Psychopathology, 11,* 607–628.

Tawney, J.W., & Gast, D.L. (1984). *Single subject research in special education.* Columbus, OH: Merrill.

Treuting, J. J., & Hinshaw, S. P., (2001). Depression and self-esteem in boys with attention-deficit/hyperactivity disorder: Associations with comorbid aggression and explanatory attributional mechanisms. *Journal of Abnormal Child Psychology, 29,* 23-39.

Ulusahin, A., Basoglu, M., & Paykel, E. S. (1994). A cross cultural comparative study of depressive symptoms in British and Turkish clinical samples. *Psychiatry Epidemiology, 9,* 29-31.

Vitaro, F., Brendgen, M., & Barker, E, D. (2006). Subtypes of aggressive behaviors: A developmental perspective. *International Journal of Behavioral Development, 30(1),* 12-19.

Vitaro, F., Tremblay, R. E., Gagnon, C., & Pelletier, D. (1994). Predictive accuracy of behavioral sociometric assessments of high-risk kindergarten children. *Journal of Clinical Child Psychology, 23*, 272-282.

Walker, H. M., Kavanagh, K., Stiller, B., Golly, A., Severson, H. H., & Feil, E. G. (1998). First Step to Success: An early intervention approach for preventing school antisocial behavior. *Journal of Emotional and Behavioral Disorders, 6*, 66-80.

Weiss, G., & Hechtman, L. (1986). *Hyperactive children grown up.* New York: Guilford Press.

Walker, H. M., Stiller, B., Golly, A., Kavanagh, K., Severson, H. H., & Feil, E. G. (1997). *First Step to Success Implementation Guide.* Longmont, CO: Sopris West.

Weinstein, S. R., Noam, G. G., Grimes, K., Stone, K., & Schwab-Stone, M. (1990). Convergence of DSM–III diagnoses and self-reported symptoms in child and adolescent inpatients. *Journal of the American Academy of Child and Adolescent, 29*, 627-634.

Wells, K. C., Epstein, J. N., Hinshaw, S. P., Conners, C. K., Klaric, J., Abikoff, H. B., et al. (2000). Parenting and family stress treatment outcomes in attention deficit hyperactivity disorder (ADHD): An empirical analysis in the MTA Study. *Journal of Abnormal Child Psychology, 28*, 543-553.

Whalen, C. K., & Henker, B. (1985). The social worlds of hyperactive children. *Clinical Psychology Review, 5*, 1-32.

Whalen, C. K., & Henker, B. (1991). The social impact of stimulant treatment for hyperactive children. *Journal of Learning Disabilities, 24*, 231-241.

Wheeler, J. & Carlson, C. L. (1994). The social functioning of children with ADD with hyperactivity and ADD without hyperactivity. *Journal of Emotional and Behavioral Disorders, 2*, 2-11.

Wissenschaftlicher Buchverlag bietet

kostenfreie

Publikation

von

wissenschaftlichen Arbeiten

Diplomarbeiten, Magisterarbeiten, Master und Bachelor Theses
sowie Dissertationen, Habilitationen und wissenschaftliche Monographien

Sie verfügen über eine wissenschaftliche Abschlußarbeit zu aktuellen oder zeitlosen
Fragestellungen, die hohen inhaltlichen und formalen Ansprüchen genügt,
und haben **Interesse an einer honorarvergüteten Publikation**?

Dann senden Sie bitte erste Informationen über Ihre Arbeit per Email
an info@vdm-verlag.de. Unser Außenlektorat meldet sich umgehend bei Ihnen.

VDM Verlag Dr. Müller Aktiengesellschaft & Co. KG
Dudweiler Landstraße 125a
D - 66123 Saarbrücken

www.vdm-verlag.de

CPSIA information can be obtained at www.ICGtesting.com
Printed in the USA
BVOW020348070113

309974BV00007B/191/P